"Many people are frustrated as they live in today's modern-day culture, feeling helpless to change it. This manual will provide prayer tools to help you make a major impact on society through contending prayer!

Prayer that Impacts the World is biblical, easy-to-understand, and sure to light a fire under your prayer life!"

> **– Cindy Jacobs**, Co-founder of Generals International, Author of *Possessing the Gates of the Enemy* and *The Power of Persistent Prayer*

"If you are a follower of Jesus, you have a mandate to impact the world—which cannot be accomplished apart from prayer. Jesus showed us what it was to live a life of prayer and change the world. Now Matt Lockett and Jared Olsen have written an incredible resource for all those who desire to strengthen their prayer life and fulfill the call on their lives.

The keys shared in *Prayer That Impacts the World* are powerful, birthed in a radical community of intercessors on the front lines. Few communities are as deeply committed to the ministry of prayer as JHOP DC. I am so grateful for the years they have sowed, as they have stood on the wall and interceded for our nation. Take the principles in this study guide and put them into practice—you will find a deeper revelation of prayer that will impact the world around you."

> **– Banning Liebscher**, Pastor of Jesus Culture, Sacramento, CA, Author of *Rooted*

"In a critical hour for our nation and the world, local churches must engage in the global prayer movement. The intercessors at Justice House of Prayer DC carry a message worth hearing.

Matt Lockett has spent many years in the nation's capital city, discovering principles of effective prayer that have proven to reshape culture and impact society. *Prayer that Impacts the World* places into your hands truths that will help you love Jesus more and step into your destiny as a world-changer."

> **– Jim Garlow**, Pastor of Skyline Church, San Diego, CA, Author of *Well Versed*

"I'm always excited about fresh manna from the throne that further enables intercessors to impact our deeply troubled culture. With a clear and concise study-outline format, *Prayer that Impacts the World* does just that.

This timely guide presents deep truths and tried-and-true methods of learning and teaching intercession—easily accessible on both a personal and corporate level. *Prayer that Impacts the World* is destined to transform hearts in personal devotion and birth deeply-rooted prayer movements that will impact our nation and the world."

> **– Dick Eastman**, International President of Every Home for Christ, Author of *Intercessory Worship* and *The Purple Pig and Other Miracles*

"Prayer should play a central role in the life of every believer. Unfortunately, it is often an arena not easily understood or clearly taught. *Prayer that Impacts the World* can be used by any believer to gain a deeper understanding of prayer. Full of biblical insights, and laid out in a practical way, this is a powerful resource for churches and small groups to use as a teaching guide.

You don't have to settle for wandering in prayer and hoping you're hitting the mark. By applying the principles in this book, you can pray in agreement with the Word of God—becoming both strategic and effective in this important endeavor."

> – **Dutch Sheets**, Author of *Intercessory Prayer* and *An Appeal To Heaven*

"For anyone with a burning heart to glorify Jesus, this guide is an extremely powerful resource to devote yourself to shaping history through prayer. The teachings have been forged in the furnace of frontline intercession for America. It is authentic, revelatory, Word-based and transformative."

> – **Faytene Grasseschi**, Founder of TheCRY Movement, Ontario, Canada

"Through prayer, believers actually partner with the God of the universe to govern the world. Matt Lockett and Jared Olsen have labored for years, living out the lessons they impart in this truly rich resource. This is an invaluable guide regardless of where you are on the journey."

> – **Joel Richardson**, Author of When a *Jew Rules the World* and *The Islamic Antichrist*

"Matt Lockett and Jared Olsen have put together a manual that will fuel your prayer life. Read it, put what you learn into practice at home, work and church—and watch God move!"

> – **Will Ford**, Director of Marketplace Leadership, Christ for the Nations Institute, Author of *Created for Influence*

"God is raising up a prayer movement in this hour! He calls us to be aware of times and seasons—how the prophetic storyline of His Word is reflected in today's headlines. Justice House of Prayer DC seeks to see that bigger picture everyday.

In this study guide, you'll learn how the government of our Sovereign King can effect change in modern-day government and culture. Let's be voices that echo on earth and in eternity!"

> – **Jennifer LeClaire**, Editor, *Charisma Magazine*, Author of *The Next Great Move of God*

"Matt Lockett and the Justice House of Prayer truly have their ear to the ground when it comes to seeking Heavenly strategies for our earthly occupation. I recommend this resource as one way to dig deeper into the Word of God and understand the power of contending prayer."

> – **Congressman Trent Franks**, Arizona, 8th District

PRAYER
that
IMPACTS
the
WORLD

A STUDY GUIDE FOR DEVELOPING
A CULTURE OF CONTENDING PRAYER

MATT LOCKETT & JARED OLSEN

Washington, DC

Published by Justice House of Prayer DC
P.O. Box 15190, Washington, DC 20003
jhopdc.com

First Edition

ISBN: 978-0-9979290-0-3

Cover design by Jared Olsen
Interior design by Matt Lockett
Editing by Josh M. Shepherd

Dedicated to small companies of believers
who pray against all odds.

"A school to teach preachers how to pray, as God counts praying, would be more beneficial to true piety, true worship, and true preaching than all theological schools."

E.M. Bounds

CONTENTS

PREFACE

The goal of this book is to reproduce among the body of Christ a desire and conviction to pursue a culture of prayer within churches, home groups, prayer networks, houses of prayer—anywhere believers gather to see the supernatural breakthrough of God's purposes in the earth.

These teachings are not mere theories. They represent core beliefs that have been developed through years of application and practical experience. Moreover, they have been put to the test in some of the most difficult situations and conditions. In other words, these are principles that have been hammered out in real-world settings.

These applications can be made on a personal level, on an increasingly larger regional scope, and even stretching into a national and an international scale.

The topic of prayer is both simple and complex. It is simple in the fact that believers enjoy an instant access to the throne of grace thanks to the sacrifice that Jesus Christ offered on our behalf. Every Christian *can* pray. At the same time, it is complex in the sense that many factors may affect the praying person's ability to effectively focus, engage multiple dimensions of opposition, and see an ultimate breakthrough by way of growing faith.

Our aim is to identify several primary issues of importance for developing a culture of prayer—more specifically one that contends for a breakthrough—whether that's in your home or in your church. This collection of teachings is by no means an exhaustive list. However, they do contain many subjects that are often overlooked or misunderstood—ones that we feel are imperative for the kind of breakthrough that so many are seeking.

The decision was made to present them in the form of outlined teaching notes with the hope that it would promote an easy study and use for small group development. The workbook format is used so that topics can be easily referenced and studied in any order, although the content is organized with a progression in mind from beginning to end.

A special emphasis is given to the priority of unity and agreement among believers. It is our desire to maximize the blessing of agreement through the teaching of these principles among praying people who are reaching for greater levels of cooperation with each other.

We want to echo the prayer of the Apostle Paul who exhorted believers, "May the God of endurance and encouragement grant you to live in such harmony with one another, in accord with Christ Jesus, that together you may with one voice glorify the God and Father of our Lord Jesus Christ." (Romans 15:5-6 ESV)

Matt Lockett- *Executive Director, Justice House of Prayer DC*
Jared Olsen- *Associate Director, International House of Prayer Tallahassee*

SECTION 1

Growing in Personal Devotion and Love Toward God

"To have found God and still to pursue him is the soul's paradox of love, scorned indeed by the too easily satisfied religionist, but justified in happy experience by the children of the burning heart."

A.W. Tozer

The Invitation to Friendship with Jesus

When we look at the early church in the book of Acts, it is easy to apply labels: they were a missional movement, a prayer movement, a healing movement, a preaching movement and more. However, the driving conviction of the early Church wasn't the vision of solely being a "movement."

Undoubtedly, something greater apprehended their hearts and motives: the uniqueness of the God-Man Jesus Christ. Jesus *was* the movement. He is the source from which justice, prayer, worship, healing, miracles, signs and wonders flows like a never-ending torrent. By examing Scripture, we see that Jesus Himself was the primary motivation of the early Church.

I. **THE NEARNESS OF CHRIST IN THE EARLY CHURCH**

A. To the disciples in the early church, a life in the Spirit and the words of Jesus were avidly *real* and *personal*. The words and remembrance of a Man stirred these weak individuals to stay in the place of friendship—through ministry to the Lord—before, during, and after the Day of Pentecost (see Acts 1; 2; 4; 13).

    29 "Brothers, I may say to you with confidence about the patriarch David that he both died and was buried, and his tomb is with us to this day. 30 Being therefore a prophet, and knowing that God had sworn with an oath to him that he would set one of his descendants on his throne, 31 he foresaw and spoke about the resurrection of the Christ, that he was not abandoned to Hades, nor did his flesh see corruption. 32 This Jesus God raised up, and of that we all are witnesses. (Acts 2:29-32 ESV)

B. Above all else, the early Church was a Christocentric movement, hungering for the revealing and knowing of Christ and Christ crucified (1 Corinthians 2:2). Friendship with Jesus through prayer *defined* their lives. It radically *disrupted* their personal agendas. It *sustained* them through the coming widespread persecution of the church.

C. Through the Person of Jesus, God released a divine wounding in the disciples' hearts that provoked a lifestyle response. They were compelled by friendship with Jesus. They longed for His presence. They hastened the Day of His return. The cry "Maranatha! Come Lord, Jesus!" became their anthem. (see Luke 12:36; 1 Corinthians 1:7; 1 Thessalonians 1:10; Titus 2:13; Jude 1:21).

D. This invitation to be a friend of Jesus was the lifeblood of their ministry. It is invitation that is still extended to believers today.

E.   Truly, if we could see what the early Church saw—the matchless worth of Jesus—we could live as they lived. The Father divinely endorses the overflow of this friendship with power, signs and wonders (Acts 4:31-33).

   1.   Subsequently, one of the primary ministries that will prepare the nations of the return of the Lord is the ministry of night and day intercession that is rooted in friendship with Jesus. God has promised to establish a global prayer movement before the appearing of His Son that will testify of what is to come.

   The one who has the bride [the body of Christ] is the bridegroom [Jesus]. The friend of the bridegroom, who stands and hears him, rejoices greatly at the bridegroom's voice. (John 3:29 ESV)

   2.   While this ministry seems strange to many in our generation, there is a profound wealth of historical and Biblical evidence that points to its power and value. (Luke 18:7-8; Matthew 21:13; 25:1-13; Isaiah 19:20-22; 24:14-16; 25:9; 26:8-9; 27:2-5, 13; 30:18-19; 42:10-13; 43:26; 51:11; 52:8; 62:6-7; Jeremiah 31:7; 51:8; Joel 2:12-17, 32; Zephaniah 2:1-3; Psalm 102:17-20; 122:6; 149:6-9; Zechariah 8:20-23; 10:1; 12:10; 13:9)

II.   DEFINING FRIENDSHIP WITH JESUS

A.   Christianity at its foundation is not simply a lifestyle, set of beliefs, moral code, or gathering around a certain cause. Christianity is an active relationship with the Person of Jesus Christ, a Person to be known, not an object to acquire information about.

B.   As a young man, extremely ill and facing the prospects of eternity, Rees Howells experienced the "plasticity" of His relationship with Christ, exclaiming:

   I found that I had only an historical Christ and not a personal Saviour who could take me to the other side.[1] –Rees Howells

C.   Currently, in the West, we have trivialized what it means to have friendship with Jesus. Many think if you say a prayer at the altar, change your morals, go to church on Sunday, you are now a Christian. As the ocean of religious ambiguity creeps in, the central plumb-line has moved away from friendship with Jesus, instead replaced by a vague and ambiguous concept of what it means to be a Christian.

D.   What does it actually mean to grow in friendship with Jesus?

---

[1] Grubb, Norman. *Rees Howells: Intercessor.* Fort Washington: Christian Literature Crusade, 1952. Print.

It wasn't a point of doctrine I saw; no it was <u>Calvary</u>. It wasn't giving a mental assent; no, the veil was taken back, my eyes were opened, and I saw <u>Him</u>.[2]
–Rees Howells

III. THREE FACETS TO THE REALITY OF FRIENDSHIP WITH CHRIST

A. We cannot lay hold of the depth of friendship with Christ that we desire unless we actually know what it is that we are in search of.

1. The invitation to friendship

   a. The revelation of God's desire for us.

   b. Pray: "God, how do you feel about me?"

      We love because He first loved us. (1 John 4:19 ESV)

2. The substance of friendship

   a. Relational knowledge is the substance of friendship.

   b. Intimacy in friendship increases as relational knowledge grows. We are most intimate with those whom we know the deepest (i.e., husband, wife, mom, dad, best friend).

3. The overflow of friendship

   a. God's heart is moved by something, therefore our heart is moved (joy, emotional transformation, obedience, devotion, etc.)

IV. RELATIONAL KNOWLEDGE

A. Our love and passion for Jesus must be rooted in the revelation of Jesus in scripture.

   [30] When he [Jesus] was at table with them, he took the bread and blessed and broke it and gave it to them. [31] And their eyes were opened, and they recognized him. And he vanished from their sight. [32] They said to each other, "<u>Did not our hearts burn within us</u> while he talked to us on the road, <u>while he opened to us the Scriptures?</u>" (Luke 24:30-32 ESV)

B. Any passion not completely anchored in Jesus' identity will be fleeting zeal and

---

[2] Grubb.

hollow sentiment. Jesus is filled with desire to open the Scriptures and reveal Himself.

1. If our passion is for a Person, our natural response would be to consume everything centered around that Person.

2. Passion for Jesus must be based around the knowledge of His life revealed in the Word. Knowledge is the fuel for love and relationship.

C. The crisis of ignorance:

1. It's becoming common to know very little about Jesus as Christianity is increasingly being defined by a belief in basic formulas, good moral ideas, participation in activities, or an allegiance to issues. Christianity has often been defined by so many things, but Christ.

2. The early Church was pierced so deeply by a revelation of Jesus that they radically reoriented every area of their lives around glorifying Him. This ravenous obsession of Jesus earned them a nickname: Christians.

And in Antioch the disciples were first called Christians. (Acts 11:26 ESV)

D. The crisis of relevance:

1. The most important issue the apostles faced was concerning the reality of the truth about Jesus. In the End-Times, the Holy Spirit will emphasize the same issue to the End-Time prophets and apostles. The question in that hour: "Who do they say Jesus is?" (Matt. 16:13-19)

13 Now when Jesus came into the district of Caesarea Philippi, he asked his disciples, "Who do people say that the Son of Man is?" 14 And they said, "Some say John the Baptist, others say Elijah, and others Jeremiah or one of the prophets." 15 He said to them, "But who do you say that I am?" (Matthew 16:13-15 ESV)

2. Jesus took the question from being a vague poll of public opinion to making it intimately personal. Who do *you* say that Jesus is?

3. Because Jesus is God His life is entirely relevant to us. We know what God is like by looking at the life of Christ.

No longer do I call you servants, for a servant does not know what his master is doing; but I have called you friends, for all things that I heard from My father I have made known to you. (John 15:15 ESV)

I have come that they may have life and have it more abundantly [to the full- NIV] (John 10:10 ESV)

V. FRIENDS OF THE BRIDEGROOM

A. Being a friend of Jesus is about much more than having good devotional times. It is about being one whom he shares his plans and burdens with.

B. John the Baptist defined his entire lifestyle and ministry around this reality of friendship with Jesus, the Bridegroom God. He was a friend of the bridegroom who stood and heard him (John 3:29). When the priests and levites asked John who he was, he declared to them Isaiah 40:3.

   A voice cries: "In the wilderness prepare the way of the Lord; make straight in the desert a highway for our God." (Isaiah 40:3 ESV)

C. Speaking in regards to Jesus, John used the proper name of God, essentially declaring, "I am preparing the way of JEHOVAH!" Every Gospel begins with this core revelation. The Holy Spirit meant to reveal everything through this lens: Jesus *is* God in flesh.

   He [Jesus] is the radiance of the glory of God and the exact imprint [representation- NIV] of his nature, and he upholds the universe by the word of his power. (Hebrews 1:3 ESV)

D. This revelation and identity of Jesus was the "piercing power" in the early Church:

   36 "Therefore let all the house of Israel know assuredly that God has made this Jesus, whom you crucified, both Lord and Christ." 37 Now when they heard this, they were cut to the heart, and said to Peter and the rest of the apostles, "Men and brethren, what shall we do?" 38 Then Peter said to them, "Repent, and let every one of you be baptized in the name of Jesus Christ for the remission of sins; and you shall receive the gift of the Holy Spirit. (Acts 2:36-38 NKJV)

E. The result of the unique identity of Jesus is that He is the fullness of the Divine nature of God. In Christ alone we find the revelation of *who God is* and *what He is like.*

F. The implications of this is that we must wholly redefine our lives around this central reality. While Jesus is often viewed as the stepping stone to enter into something higher, the Father is intent on glorifying His Son that He would have preeminence in all things (Colossians 1:17-18; Isaiah 2:10-11; Hebrews 1).

VI. CALLED TO STAND AND HEAR AS FRIENDS

A. Scripture records three times in the New Testament when the Father speaks audibly to Jesus:

1. At the baptism of Christ:

   and the Holy Spirit descended on him in bodily form, like a dove; and a voice came from heaven, "You are my beloved Son; with you I am well pleased." (Luke 3:22 ESV)

2. When some said it thundered:

   [28] "Father, glorify your name." Then a voice came from heaven: "I have glorified it, and I will glorify it again." [29] The crowd that stood there and heard it said that it had thundered. Others said, "An angel has spoken to him." [30] Jesus answered, "This voice has come for your sake, not mine. (John 12:28-30 ESV)

3. At Jesus' Transfiguration:

   [5] He was still speaking when, behold, a bright cloud overshadowed them, and a voice from the cloud said, "This is my beloved Son, with whom I am well pleased..." (Matthew 17:5 ESV)

B. Yet there is only one time that Scripture records the Father speaking audibly to others, also at His Transfiguration (Matthew 17:5; Luke 9:35).

   [5] He was still speaking when, behold, a bright cloud overshadowed them, and a voice from the cloud said, "This is my beloved Son, with whom I am well pleased; listen to him." (Matthew 17:5 ESV)

   [1] And after six days Jesus took with him Peter and James, and John his brother, and led them up a high mountain by themselves. [2] And he was transfigured before them, and his face shone like the sun, and his clothes became white as light. [3] And behold, there appeared to them Moses and Elijah, talking with him. [4] And Peter said to Jesus, "Lord, it is good that we are here. If you wish, I will make three tents here, one for you and one for Moses and one for Elijah." [5] He was still speaking when, behold, a bright cloud overshadowed them, and a voice from the cloud said, "This is my beloved Son, with whom I am well pleased; listen to him." [6] When the disciples heard this, they fell on their faces and were terrified. [7] But Jesus came and touched them, saying, "Rise, and have no fear." [8] And when they lifted up their eyes, they saw no one but Jesus only. (Matthew 17:1-8 ESV)

C.   The Father implores Peter, James and John to "listen" to Jesus alone. Jesus was not simply another rabbi, prophet or teacher like Moses or Elijah. He was unique in that He was the God-Man. His unique identity demands cultivating a listening ear to His words as His friends.

D.   Friendship with Jesus finds its fullest expression through the First Commandment lifestyle. It is dynamically connected to *hearing* His voice (abiding in the Vine) and *doing* His will (following His commands).

1.   When the First Commandment is put in first place, the Second Commandment becomes anointed and a baptism of power is released. Thus, we must have discernment on what is primary, the First Commandment, and what is secondary, the Second Commandment. The two cannot be divorced from one another.

2.   That which Jesus established through the early Church at His first coming, the Holy Spirit will restore prior to his Second Coming. God is sovereignly releasing this invitation: who will be a friend of the Bridegroom at the end of the age?

The Spirit and the bride say, "Come!" (Revelation 22:17 NIV)

Cultivating a Burning Heart

What is the ultimate goal of the Church? Most believers would agree that the ultimate goal of the Church should be an earnest reflection of the ultimate goal in God's heart.

We must discover what is the ultimate goal in God's heart in time and eternity. Endeavoring to answer that question has profound implications.

> *If God desires every knee to bow to Jesus and every tongue to confess Him, so should we. We should be 'jealous' for the honor of His name—troubled when it remains unknown, hurt when it is ignored, indignant when it is blasphemed, and all the time anxious and determined that it shall be given the honor and glory which are due to it.*

> *The highest of all missionary motives is neither obedience to the Great Commission (important as that is), nor love for sinners who are alienated and perishing (strong as that incentive is, especially when we contemplate the wrath of God), but rather zeal—burning and passionate zeal—for the glory of Jesus Christ.*

> *Only one imperialism is Christian, and that is concern for His Imperial Majesty Jesus Christ, and for the glory of his empire or kingdom. Before this supreme goal of the Christian mission, all unworthy motives wither and die.[1] –John Stott*

Responding to God's beckoning and remaining faithful for decades does not happen automatically. Thanfully, God has a sovereign plan to help believers cultivate a burning heart for His glory. If God's ultimate goal is to uphold, display and exalt the glory of His name in all the earth, then encountering the glory of God carries unprecedented *value* and *significance* to a believers calling.

I.   THE CHIEF END IN GOD'S HEART

    A.   Beholding the glory of God in the face of Jesus Christ is the fulfillment of the Godhead's desires.

        1.   The chief desire in God's heart is not just for humanities needs to be met, but that the nations would sing of His glory and revere His name throughout the earth.

> **For from the rising of the sun to its setting my name will be great among the nations, and in every place incense will be offered to my name, and a pure offering. For my name will be great among the nations, says the LORD of hosts. (Malachi 1:11 ESV)**

---

[1] Stott, John. *Romans: God's Good News for the World.* Downers Grover: InterVarsity Press, 1994. Print.

Missions is not the ultimate goal of the church. Worship is. Missions exists because worship doesn't. Worship is ultimate, not missions, because God is ultimate, not man. When this age is over, and the countless millions of the redeemed fall on their faces before the throne of God, missions will be no more. It is a temporary necessity. But worship abides forever.[2] –John Piper

2. The chief end in God's heart is that a people from every tribe, language, people group and nation would be redeemed to glorify God by worshipping Jesus forever.

B. Today in the West we find a generation with a multitude of options, choices, freedoms, opinions, and technologies. Almost anything can communicated, bought, or discovered at the click of a button or swipe of the finger. Ironically, we are being entertained by more and more of less and less. Consequentially, many of today's young church planters are being churned out across America, taught that if you want to truly impact this generation you must make the gospel relevant and presentable. However, if this generation is perishing, it is not perishing for a lack of novel methodologies and relevant presentation. Just as it was in Jeremiah's day, so it is in ours:

...But my people have changed their glory for that which does not profit. (Jeremiah 2:11)

C. The glory of God is what the human heart was made to *see* and enjoy for all of eternity. Jesus hung upon that jagged Cross so that weak and broken humanity might be redeemed to experience this.

II. THE DESIRE OF CHRIST

A. John 17 takes place before Jesus' death in light of the Cross. After speaking to His disciples and praying that they would not fall away amidst the coming shakings of His death and the future persecution of the saints (Acts 8:1-2), Jesus sets His eyes on the future ingathering of all believers through the Church's and the apostles bold witness.

"I do not ask for these only, but also <u>for those who will believe in me</u> through their word..." (John 17:20 ESV)

[24] "Father, I desire that they also, whom you have given me, may...see my glory that you have given me because you loved me before the foundation of the world... [26] I made known to them your name, and I will continue to make it known, that the love with which you have loved me may be in them, and I in

---

[2] Piper, John. *Let the Nations Be Glad!: The Supremacy of God in Missions*. Grand Rapids: Baker Academic, 2010. Print.

them." (John 17:24,26 ESV)

1. When Jesus prayed the High Priestly prayer, the groan of His intercession essentially was this: "Father, if I go to the Cross, I want something more than worker-bees! I want something more than a project to make Me look good! I want them to experience the depths of Our glory and love forever! I want to be one with them and they with Me!"

2. Jesus was interceding from the place of *desire* for the future promise of all believers becoming One in Christ, beholding His glory, and encountering the truth that the Father loves them as much as He loves Jesus.

3. The ultimate prayer in Jesus' heart was for the Father to "glorify the Son" (v. 1) by causing belieivers to "see" (v.24) Jesus' glory, the glory of the Godhead that Jesus had "before the world existed" (v. 5). This "glory" is a gift "given" (v. 22) to us by Jesus from the Father for the sake of glorifying Him.

B. We have to understand how tenacious God is for His own glory and that of the Godhead. Passion for His Son Jesus burns brightly in the Father's heart and He is fiercely committed to exalting it above every other thing.

C. Jesus' prayer is still being answered. Even now the Father is answering it, releasing Divine ambushes across the earth with His desires for us and for His own glory and exaltation.

III. WHAT IS THE GLORY OF GOD?

A. Ask yourself these searching questions: What produces the inward experience? How does authentic heart transformation take place? What compels desire for Jesus and causes one to voluntarily lay down their life for Him like bondservants? What provokes boldness to proclaim Him to others?

[17] Now the Lord is the Spirit, and where the Spirit of the Lord is, there is freedom. [18] And we all, with unveiled face, beholding the glory of the Lord, are being transformed into the same image from one degree of glory to another. (2 Corinthians 3:17-18 ESV)

B. In 2 Corinthians 3:18, Paul was declaring that transformation takes place in the heart of men, not just by changing our actions, but by *beholding* something—the glory of God. Undoubtedly, that which we behold—that which we set our mind, eyes, and spirit upon—we become like.

C. Beholding God's glory is the source of inward experience, that which produces a life of godliness and the never-ending fuel of prayer, missions, and obedience to Jesus.

IV. THE REVEALING OF GOD'S GLORY

A. Moses beheld God's glory.

¹⁸ Moses said, "Please show me your glory." ¹⁹ And he said, "I will make all my goodness pass before you and will proclaim before you my name 'The Lord.' And I will be gracious to whom I will be gracious, and will show mercy on whom I will show mercy. ²⁰ But," he said, "you cannot see my face, for man shall not see me and live." ²¹ And the Lord said, "Behold, there is a place by me where you shall stand on the rock, ²² and while my glory passes by I will put you in a cleft of the rock, and I will cover you with my hand until I have passed by. ²³ Then I will take away my hand, and you shall see my back, but my face shall not be seen." (Exodus 33:18-23 ESV)

1. God answers Moses' request. This is God revealing God to the human heart.

    ⁵ The Lord descended in the cloud and stood with him there, and proclaimed the name of the Lord. ⁶ The Lord passed before him and proclaimed, "The Lord, the Lord, a God <u>merciful</u> and <u>gracious,</u> <u>slow to anger,</u> and <u>abounding in steadfast love and faithfulness,</u> ⁷ <u>keeping steadfast love for thousands,</u> <u>forgiving</u> iniquity and transgression and sin, but who will <u>by no means clear the guilty</u> [release of justice]..." ⁸ And Moses quickly bowed his head toward the earth and worshiped. (Exodus 34:5-8 ESV)

2. Moses beholds God's glory and records *who* He is in His nature, *what* He is like in His character, and *how* He feels about us in the way the He relates to us. God declares to Moses that His glory is His goodness and His name—it's His goodness, kindness, graciousness, mercy, forgiveness, justice, zeal, and more.

3. The revelation of God's glory produces a response of humility and worship in Moses.

B. Our emotional DNA changes when we come into contact with who God is and how He feels about us.

V. MESSENGERS OF GLORY

A. External reforms alone will never produce the inward transformation that is needed.

B. The primary way to raise up disciples is to get them to behold the glory of God. God has called the redeemed to behold His glory.

His divine power has granted to us all things that pertain to life and godliness, through the knowledge of him who <u>called us to his own glory</u> and excellence... (2 Peter 1:3 ESV)

[11] In him we have obtained an inheritance, having been predestined according to the purpose of him who works all things according to the counsel of his will, [12] so that we who were the first to hope in Christ might be <u>to the praise of his glory</u>. (Ephesians 1:11-12 ESV)

C. What comes into your mind when you think about God?

What comes into our minds when we think about God is the most important thing about us. The history of mankind will probably show that no people has ever risen above its religion... that no religion has ever been greater than its idea of God. Worship is pure or base as the worshiper entertains high or low thoughts of God.

For this reason the gravest question before the Church is always God Himself, and the most portentous fact about any man is not what he at a given time may say or do, but what he in his deep heart conceives God to be like. We tend by a secret law of the soul to move toward our mental image of God. This is true not only of the individual Christian, but of the company of Christians that composes the Church. Always the most revealing thing about the Church is her idea of God, just as her most significant message is what she says about Him or leaves unsaid, for her silence is often more eloquent than her speech. She can never escape the self-disclosure of her witness concerning God.

The low view of God entertained almost universally among Christians is the cause of a hundred lesser evils everywhere among us... with our loss of the sense of majesty has come the further loss of religious awe and consciousness of the divine Presence.[3] –A.W. Tozer

D. Right thinking produces right feeling produces right acting.

1. If we are transformed into the likeness of that which we behold, then if we wrongly behold God's character to be mostly stingy, frustrated, angry, and passive, for example, then we will live stingy, frustrated, angry, and disengaged from cooperating with God.

---

[3] Tozer, A. W. *The Knowledge of the Holy: The Attributes of God, Their Meaning in the Christian Life.* New York: Harper & Row, 1961. Print.

2. There is an engrossing problem that counteracts right thinking: mankind's sin nature.

    ... for all have sinned and fall short of the glory of God... (Romans 3:23 ESV)

    And the Word became flesh and dwelt among us, and we have seen his glory... (John 1:14 ESV)

    [3] And even if our gospel is veiled, it is veiled only to those who are perishing. [4] In their case the god of this world [Satan] has blinded the minds of the unbelievers, to keep them from seeing the light of the gospel of the glory of Christ, who is the image of God. (2 Corinthians 4:3-4 ESV)

E. There is a full-scale war against the glory of God.

    1. Satan's objective is to make the glory of God appear foggy and muddled. Satan is responsible for this blindness in concert with humanities depravity. Satan led humanity astray in the Garden with Adam and Eve, but humanity did it in concert with Satan's leadership.

    2. While God's primary objective is to be glorified, Satan's primary objective is to mock, belittle, and distort the glory of God.

    3. Satan's work is thwarted when God speaks the light of the gospel into a darkened world through intercessors and messengers.

F. What is the gospel? What is the good news? Paul declared that the "light of the gospel" is the "glory of Christ."

    The heaviest obligation lying upon the Christian Church today is to purify and elevate her concept of God until it is once more worthy of Him - and of her. In all her prayers and labors this should have first place. We do the greatest service to the next generation of Christians by passing on to them undimmed and undiminished that noble concept of God which we received from our Hebrew and Christian fathers of generations past.[4] -A.W. Tozer

VI. DOES YOUR HEART BURN WITHIN YOU?

A. Does your heart burn within you at thoughts of the glory of Jesus?

    [13] That very day two of them were going to a village named Emmaus, about seven miles from Jerusalem, [14] and they were talking with each other about all these

---

[4] Tozer.

things that had happened. ¹⁵ While they were talking and discussing together, Jesus himself drew near and went with them. ¹⁶ But their eyes were kept from recognizing him. ¹⁷ And he said to them, "What is this conversation that you are holding with each other as you walk?" And they stood still, looking sad. ¹⁸ Then one of them, named Cleopas, answered him, "Are you the only visitor to Jerusalem who does not know the things that have happened there in these days?" ¹⁹ And he said to them, "What things?" And they said to him, "Concerning Jesus of Nazareth, a man who was a prophet mighty in deed and word before God and all the people, ²⁰ and how our chief priests and rulers delivered him up to be condemned to death, and crucified him. ²¹ But we had hoped that he was the one to redeem Israel. Yes, and besides all this, it is now the third day since these things happened. ²² Moreover, some women of our company amazed us. They were at the tomb early in the morning, ²³ and when they did not find his body, they came back saying that they had even seen a vision of angels, who said that he was alive. ²⁴ Some of those who were with us went to the tomb and found it just as the women had said, but him [Jesus] they did not see." ²⁵ And he [Jesus] said to them, "O foolish ones, and slow of heart to believe all that the prophets have spoken! ²⁶ Was it not necessary that the Christ should suffer these things and enter into his glory?" ²⁷ <u>And beginning with Moses and all the Prophets, he interpreted to them in all the Scriptures the things concerning himself.</u> (Luke 24:13-27 ESV)

³² They said to each other, <u>"Did not our hearts burn within us while he talked to us on the road, while he opened to us the Scriptures?"</u> ³³ And they rose that same hour and returned to Jerusalem. And they found the eleven and those who were with them gathered together, ³⁴saying, "The Lord has risen indeed, and has appeared to Simon!" ³⁵ Then they told what had happened on the road, and how he was known to them in the breaking of the bread. (Luke 24:32-35 ESV)

B.   It was the revelation of the glory of Jesus "in all the Scriptures" that caused disciples hearts to burn. Throughout Scripture, Jesus' nature and character is often likened to fire.

1.   Ezekiel's testimony:

²⁶ And above the expanse over their heads there was the likeness of a throne, in appearance like sapphire; and seated above the likeness of a throne was a likeness with a human appearance. ²⁷ And upward from what had the appearance of his waist I saw as it were gleaming metal, <u>like the appearance of fire</u> enclosed all around. And downward from what had the appearance of his waist I saw as it were <u>the appearance of fire</u>, and there was brightness around him. ²⁸ ... <u>Such was the appearance of the likeness of the glory of the Lord.</u> (Ezekiel 1:26-28 ESV)

2. John's testimony:

    His eyes are like a <u>flame of fire</u>, and on his head are many diadems, and he has a name written that no one knows but himself. (Revelation 19:12 ESV)

3. Paul's testimony:

    And then the lawless one will be revealed, whom the Lord will consume with the breath of His mouth and destroy with <u>the brightness</u> of His coming. (2 Thessalonians 2:8 NKJV)

4. Malachi's testimony:

    ² ...For He is like a <u>refiner's fire</u> and like launderers' soap. ³ He will sit as a <u>refiner</u> and a purifier of silver; He will purify the sons of Levi, and purge them as gold and silver... ⁶ "For I am the Lord, I do not change; therefore you are not consumed, O sons of Jacob. (Malachi 3:2-3, 6 ESV)

C. If we are called to proclaim, not ourselves, but the glory of Christ, we must continually encounter His glory and delight in it. A burning heart is cultivated by coming into continual contact with the glory of God in the Man Christ Jesus.

    God is glorified not only by his glory's being seen, but by its being rejoiced in. . . . [W]hen those that see it delight in it: God is more glorified than if they only see it; his glory is then received by the whole soul, both by the understanding and by the heart.

    God made the world that he might communicate, and the creature receive, his glory; and that it might [be] received both by the mind and heart. He that testifies his idea of God's glory [doesn't] glorify God so much as he that testifies also his approbation of it and his delight in it.⁵ -Jonathan Edwards

D. The Father's intentions are far more glorious than giving us the right set of Bible facts to pass the test and enter Heaven. Jesus is still taking believers on the spiritual road to Emmaus to forge burning hearts in the redeemed.

E. As created beings, our reason for existence, our calling, our greatest privilege is to make visible the glory of God.

    All that is ever spoken of in the Scripture as an ultimate end of God's works is included in that one phrase, the glory of God... The refulgence shines upon and into the creature, and is reflected back to the luminary. The beams of

---

⁵ Edwards, Jonathan, and Thomas A. Schafer. *The "Miscellanies": The Works of Jonathan Edwards Series, Volume 13.* New Haven: Yale UP, 1994. Print.

glory come from God, and are something of God and are refunded back again to their original. So that the whole is of God, and in God, and to God, and God is the beginning, middle and end in this affair.[6] *-Jonathan Edwards*

F. Jesus desires believers to minister in the same way that He ministers: as ones with "burning hearts" who "bear witness to the Light" (John 1:8) with an *inward purity* that overflows in *outward righteousness* (acts of love, compassion, justice that exalts Jesus).

G. Why does Jesus desire this?

1. Inward purity: The forefront agenda in the Father's heart for our lives is primarily to cultivate greater intimacy with the Father, Son, and Holy Spirit.

2. Outward righteousness: Secondarily, God's agenda for our lives it that we would cultivate meekness before men.

    He [John the Baptist] was a burning and shining lamp, and you were willing to rejoice for a while in his light. (John 5:35 ESV)

    For the earth will be filled with the knowledge of the glory of the Lord as the waters cover the sea. (Habakkuk 2:14 ESV)

---

[6] Edwards, Jonathan. *The Dissertation Concerning the End for Which God Created the World, in The Works of Jonathan Edwards, vol. 8.* Yale University Press, 1989. Print.

The Necessity of Abiding in Christ

Jesus modeled a life of constant abiding in the presence of the Father. Time and time again, He would declare that He only did what He saw His Father in heaven doing. Time and time again, He would withdraw Himself to be alone with God.

If Jesus lived in this state of constant dependence upon God, how much more do we need to do the same? If we are to expect the transforming power of Christ to operate through our lives, then it is imperative that we understand and posture our lives to abide in Christ.

I.   THE FIRST PRIORITY IN GOD'S HEART

    A.   The first priority in God's heart relating to believers is to make the First Commandment first place in a believer's life. This includes receiving God's love, loving God in return, loving ourselves in God's love (seeing ourselves as God sees us), and loving others as God loves us.

    B.   The first agenda on the mind of the Holy Spirit is to empower our hearts for this ultimate reality—to live as Jesus lived—by the Holy Spirit living through us. Jesus referred to this as "abiding in love."

        And he said to him, "You __shall__ love the Lord your God with all your __heart__ and with all your __soul__ and with all your __mind__." (Matthew 22:37 ESV)

        If you __abide in me__, and __my words abide in you__, ask whatever you wish, and it will be done for you. (John 15:7 ESV)

    C.   Salvation is an invitation to participate in deep fellowship with the Godhead. We are not just saved *from* something, but *unto* something. Salvation is much more than just escaping Hell.

        And this is eternal life, __that they know you__ the only true God, and Jesus Christ whom you have sent. (John 17:3 ESV)

    D.   Jesus modeled a life of deep abiding in the Father and Spirit. He grew in wisdom and stature, though He was fully God and fully man (Luke 2:52). He embraced the meekness and humility of abiding by casting total dependence on the Father.

        So Jesus said to them, "Truly, truly, I say to you, __the Son can do nothing of his own accord, but only what he sees the Father doing__. For whatever the Father does, that the Son does likewise." (John 5:19 ESV)

So Jesus said to them, "When you have lifted up the Son of Man, then you will know that I am he, and that <u>I do nothing on my own authority, but speak just as the Father taught me</u>." (John 8:28 ESV)

John [the Baptist] answered, "A person cannot receive even one thing unless it is given him from heaven." (John 3:27 ESV)

E. As imagebearers, we were created with a divine capacity to receive God's affections. From that reality, we are called to interact with the One who sits on an unshakeable Throne. God releases His supernatural grace to enter into a place of ever deeper abiding with His burning heart.

II. CALLED TO ABIDE

A. Jesus calls His disciples to *abide* (or remain) *in His love*. Abiding in love involves constant encounter. The redeemed, like Jesus, are born from heaven above.

B. Jesus defined loving God as being deeply rooted in a spirit of obedience (Jn. 14:15, 21, 23; Deut. 6:1-9). There is no such thing as loving God without seeking to obey His Word.

As the Father has loved me, so have I loved you. Abide in my love. (John 15:9 ESV)

"If you love me, you will keep my commandments." (John 14:15 ESV)

C. The Holy Spirit glorifies Christ not only by what He reveals, but by what He overturns in our lives and in society.

I have been crucified with Christ. <u>It is no longer I who live, but Christ who lives in me</u>. And the life I now live in the flesh I live by faith in the Son of God, who loved me and gave himself for me. (Galatians 2:20 ESV)

> *I saw that by His coming in to me, He would love sinners through me, as He loved me. It would not be forcing myself to love others, any more than the Savior forced Himself to love me...If I live in the realm where He is, I live to have mercy, and to be kind, to love others...I had left the world and its folly, and been born into that Kingdom where there is only the love of God—the most attractive life on the face of the earth.[1] –Rees Howells*

III. THE PROMISED ENCOUNTER

A. Many believers are unfortunately living spiritually stifled lives without even

---

[1] Grubb, Norman. *Rees Howells: Intercessor*. Fort Washington: Christian Literature Crusade, 1952. Print.

knowing it. They have settled for a partial view of salvation, often unaware that Jesus promises an encounter with the Father Himself to the one who abides in Him.

"Whoever has my [Jesus] commandments and keeps them, he it is who loves me. And he who loves me will be loved by my Father, and I will love him and <u>manifest myself to him</u>." (John 14:21 ESV)

[20] "I do not ask for these only, but also for <u>those who will believe in me</u> through their word, [21] that they may all be one, <u>just as you, Father, are in me, and I in you</u>, that they also may be in us, so that the world may believe that you have sent me. (John 17:20-21 ESV)

B. John 17 is the bedrock of unshakeable intercession and willing partnership. In prayer, Jesus triumphantly declares that the Father loves us just as much as He loves Jesus, His own Beloved Son. We will boldly approach the throne of grace when we know that God loves us as much as God loves Jesus.

   1. When one encounters the depth of God's love, they don't view His commandments as burdens, but delights.

   2. The one who sets their hearts to love God completely and obey His Word engages in the deepest act of spiritual warfare.

IV. THE NECESSITY OF ABIDING

A. The necessity for abiding is demonstrated in the fact that the life is in the Vine. Only as the branch remains united to Jesus the Vine by abiding in Him, will His supernatural life produce fruit through believers as the branch.

Abide in me, and I in you. As the branch cannot bear fruit by itself, unless it abides in the vine, neither can you, unless you abide in me. (John 15:4 ESV)

   1. In John 14-17, Jesus' words on abiding were to prepare His disciples to walk through the greatest hour of crisis during the crucifixion events—for defection from within and persecution from without.

   2. The disciples denials and trials immediately around the crucifixion events exposed the areas of their lives where they had yet surrendered to abiding in Christ. Jesus was declaring that abiding in Him was of the highest priority to enter into the hour of crisis. Pruning is a redemptive part of abiding to conform us to Christ and bear more fruit (John 15:2).

   3. The Father brings us through trials to open our eyes to see that the

power is in Jesus Christ, not ourselves.

4. Trials cause men to confront their weakness and utter inability to bring about change apart from God. If responded to rightly, they are one of the greatest gifts from God.

    "The Christian often tries to forget his weakness; God wants us to remember it, to feel it deeply. The Christian wants to conquer his weakness and to be freed from it; God wants us to rest and even rejoice in it. The Christian mourns over his weakness; Christ teaches His servant to say, 'I take pleasure in infirmities. Most gladly ...will I...glory in my infirmities' (2 Cor. 12:9)' The Christian thinks his weaknesses are his greatest hindrance in the life and service of God; God tells us that it is the secret of strength and success. It is our weakness, heartily accepted and continually realized, that gives our claim and access to the strength of Him who has said, 'My strength is made perfect in weakness"[2] -Andrew Murray

5. God is looking for intercessors who will remain united to Him by abiding in Him so that His power will operate through the intercessor and accomplish what needs to be done.

B. Hudson Taylor's experience of learning to abide in Christ:

    "[The need for your prayer] has never been greater than at present. Envied by some, despised by many, hated by others, often blamed for things I never heard of or had nothing to do with, an innovator on what have become established rules of missionary practice, an opponent of mighty systems of heathen error and superstition, working without precedent in many respects and with few experienced helpers, often sick in body as well as perplexed in mind and embarrassed by circumstances—had not the Lord been specially gracious to me, had not my mind been sustained by the conviction that the work is His and that He is with me, . . . I must have fainted or broken down. But the battle is the Lord's, and He will conquer.

    We may fail—do fail continually—but He never fails... I have continually to mourn that I follow at such a distance and learn so slowly to imitate my precious Master. I can not tell you how I am buffeted sometimes by temptation. I never knew how bad a heart I have. Yet I do know that I love God and love His work, and desire to serve Him only and in all things. And I value above all else that precious Saviour in whom alone I can be accepted. Often I am tempted to think that one so full of sin can not be a child of God at all... May God help me to love Him more and serve Him better."[3]

---

[2] Murray, Andrew. Abide in Christ: The Joy of Being in God's Presence. Springdale, Penn.: Whitaker House, 1979. Print.
[3] Taylor, Dr. and Mrs. Howard. *Hudson Taylor's Spiritual Secret.* Chicago: Moody, 2009. Print.

From the consciousness of union springs the power to abide... Union is not identical with abiding: union is uninterrupted, but abiding may be interrupted. If abiding be interrupted, sin follows.[4]

Communion with Christ requires our coming to Him. Meditating upon His person and His work requires the diligent use of the means of grace, and specially the prayerful reading of His Word. Many fail to abide because they habitually fast instead of feed.[5] –Hudson Taylor

C.   Taylor makes a profound point. He wasn't speaking against fasting. Rather, he was stating that It is not enough to simply abstain. It is imperative that we are being filled by God's Word.

D.   Jesus connected the expectation of answered prayer to the place of abiding in His love and in having His words abide in us. Jesus is releasing an implicit call to every believer here.

If you abide in me, and my words abide in you, <u>ask whatever you wish, and it will be done for you</u>. (John 15:7 ESV)

1.   Norman Grubb wrote about the necessity Rees Howells placed upon abiding in Christ through God's Word in regards to answered prayer.

The way Mr. Howells maintained this abiding was by spending a set time of waiting upon God every day during the period in which the intercession lasted. The Holy Spirit would then speak to him through the Word, revealing any standard that he was to come up to, particularly in "the laws of the Kingdom"—the Sermon on the Mount. Any command the Spirit gave him, he must fulfill, because the way of abiding is the keeping of His commandments (John 15:10). The Spirit would also search his heart and throw light on his daily life, revealing any motives or actions that needed confession and cleansing in the Blood. But the Spirit's dealings were not so much with outward shortcomings as with the self-nature out of which they sprang. Any transgression was never to be repeated, but specific obedience on that point would be called for until a radical inward change was effected. He was "purified... in obeying the truth through the Spirit". (1 Peter 1:22.) He could never come into God's presence unless he had obeyed all that had been given him on the previous day.[6] –Norman Grubb

As Mr. Howells would continue in this place of abiding day by day, he would be

[4] Taylor, James Hudson. *Hudson Taylor's Choice Sayings: A Compilation from His Writings and Addresses.* London: China Inland Mission, 1905. Print.
[5] Taylor, Dr. and Mrs. Howard.
[6] Grubb.

increasingly conscious that the Spirit was engaging the enemy in battle and overcoming him, until finally he would become fully assured of the victory. The Spirit would then tell him that the intercession was finished, the position gained, and he would await the visible deliverance in praise and faith.[7] – Norman Grubb

2. At the end of the age, there will be a widespread emergence of false teachers and false prophets—ones who distort the word of God, intentionally or unintentionally.

    And now, little children, <u>abide in him</u>, so that <u>when he appears we may have confidence</u> and not shrink from him in shame at his coming. (1 John 2:28 ESV)

    If you abide in me, and <u>my words</u> abide in you... (John 15:7 ESV)

    The Holy Ghost rides in the chariot of Scripture, and not in the wagon of modern thought.[8] –Charles Spurgeon

3. The most practical instruction the Spirit gave to Jeremiah, Ezekiel and John the Beloved in light of their transitional generation events was to "eat the scroll." (Revelation 10:10; Ezekiel 3:3; Jeremiah 15:16).

E. The outer life of the intercessor should consist of perpetual faithful ministry that can be accounted for by their inward love for the Word.

    Your words were found, and <u>I ate them</u>, and <u>your words became to me a joy and the delight of my heart</u>, for I am called by your name, O Lord, God of hosts. (Jeremiah 15:16 ESV)

    Open my eyes, that I may behold wondrous things out of your law. (Psalm 119:18 ESV)

V. "PERFECT" ABIDING: CONDITIONS OF INTERCESSION

A. God calls us to walk in all of the light that we receive, especially in relation to Spirit-led intercession. Prayer is meant to be answered. Faith is meant to become substance. Rees Howells called this, *"a daily obedience, a daily abiding, a daily going through."*

    The Lord kept me daily and hourly abiding to fulfill the condition for claiming

---

[7] Grubb.

[8] Spurgeon, Charles. *The Metropolitan Tabernacle Pulpit. Sermons Preached and Revised By C. H. Spurgeon 1891*. Vol. 37. Print.

an answer to my prayers.⁹ –Rees Howells

There are degrees and stages of abiding. The deeper the oneness, the more the power of the risen life of Christ can operate through the channel, and new positions of spiritual authority be gained. Rees Howells' abiding was always according to the light given up to that time. In that sense abiding in a particular period could be called 'perfect,' and the victory claimed although there would still be further ways in which he was to become more like the Savior.¹⁰ –Norman Grubb

B.   Abiding does not add to our salvation, which is by grace through faith alone. However, it is the evidence of supernatural transformation taking place in the heart.

C.   Jesus attributed the Pharisees' lack of authority to their failure to abide in God's word.

...and <u>you do not have his word abiding in you</u>, for you do not believe the one [Jesus] whom he [the Father] has sent. (John 5:38 ESV)

D.   The Pharisees did not have fellowship with the Holy Spirit. They had tremendous knowledge of the Scriptures, but Jesus' words did not abide in them. They did not embrace the intimacy, humility and servanthood of intercession. Consequently, they did not possess spiritual authority. Instead of opening spiritual doors for the masses, they actually kept the masses out of the kingdom because of spiritual pride, envy and selfish ambition.

³¹ So Jesus said to the Jews who had believed him, "<u>If you abide in my word, you are truly my disciples</u>, ³² and you will know the truth, and the truth will set you free." (John 8:31-32 ESV)

"But woe to you, scribes and Pharisees, hypocrites! For you shut the kingdom of heaven in people's faces. For you neither enter yourselves nor allow those who would enter to go in. (Matthew 23:13 ESV)

E.   God desires more than just imputed righteousness. He wants to manifest the righteousness of Christ through our lives as we abide in Him.

F.   We will only walk in the power of the Holy Spirit to the degree that we talk and fellowship with the Spirit.

¹ If then you have been raised with Christ, seek the things that are above, where

---

⁹ Grubb.
¹⁰ Grubb.

Christ is, seated at the right hand of God. ² Set your minds on things that are above, not on things that are on earth. ³ For you have died, and your life is hidden with Christ in God. ⁴ When Christ who is your life appears, then you also will appear with him in glory. (Colossians 3:1-4 ESV)

Bondservants of Jesus Christ

Who will be capable of obedience when it matters most? Sadly, those who casually say they will follow the Master wherever he goes usually haven't really been tested. We must come to a place of total surrender.

The Apostle Paul said, "I have learned the secret of being content in any and every situation" (Philippians 4:10-19 NIV). We too must discover this secret as others have who have gone before us.

Once example is Rees Howells who learned the secret while under the extreme conditions of World War I, the Great Depression, and World War II. The biography Rees Howells: Intercessor recounts the difficulty of obedience in those days:

> *The day came when he reached his last pound. The Holy Spirit then told him, "Cut the ropes and take the promises." It was a direct call to step out on God. But it is always easier to talk of such things than actually to do them. It had been much easier to give £100 out of plenty, than to part with this last £1 and come to the end of his savings—for the first time in fifteen years. "Oh, how the devil pitied me, and brought such arguments!" he said. "He told me it would be a step in the dark, and that if there was a convention or anything of that kind, I wouldn't be able to go, unless I had £1 laid by. But the Holy Ghost showed me that if God wanted me to go anywhere, He would surely provide the means. The danger was on the other side: for while a person has money, he can go without consulting God, like Jonah, who could afford to pay his passage to run away from Him! The fact is, we can never really be bondservants until God does control our means."[1]*
> *–Norman Grubb*

I.   STEPPING INTO YOUR IDENTITY IN CHRIST

   A.   There has been an undeniable emphasis in recent years throughout the body of Christ on rediscovering our identity as *sons* and entering into the confidence and rest of sonship.

   > *[26] For in Christ Jesus you are all sons of God, through faith. [27] For as many of you as were baptized into Christ have put on Christ... [1] I mean that the heir, as long as he is a child, is no different from a slave, though he is the owner of everything, [2] but he is under guardians and managers until the date set by his father. [3] In the same way we also, when we were children, were enslaved to the elementary principles of the world. [4] But when the fullness of time had come, God sent forth his Son, born of woman, born under the law, [5] to redeem those who were under the law, so that we might receive adoption as sons. [6] And*

---

[1] Grubb, Norman. *Rees Howells: Intercessor.* Fort Washington: Christian Literature Crusade, 1952. Print.

because you are sons, God has sent the Spirit of his Son into our hearts, crying, "Abba! Father!" [7] *So <u>you are no longer a slave, but a son</u>, and if a son, then an heir through God. (Galatians 3:26-27, 4:1-7 ESV)*

B. This is a message that truly brings healing, freedom, and deliverance from dead works and harmful mindsets. This kind of intimacy with God must be restored as the primary revelation, motivation, and focus for our lives.

C. Some confusion is possible, though, when we are challenged to walk out sonship the way Christ modeled it.

[5] Have this mind among yourselves, which is yours in Christ Jesus, [6] who, though he was in the form of God, did not count equality with God a thing to be grasped, [7] but emptied himself, by taking the form of <u>a servant</u> [Greek: doulos], being born in the likeness of men. [8] And being found in human form, he <u>humbled himself</u> by becoming obedient to the point of death, even death on a cross. (Philippians 2:5-8 ESV)

D. The Son came—the one fully confident in his identity—and yet he made himself a slave; a *doulos (pronounced dü'-los)*.

E. In various translations, *doulos* is rendered as "servant" or "slave." It is best translated as "bondservant" or "bond-man"[2] in its historical context, although those are unfamiliar words in this day and age.

   1. In the first century, it is estimated that approximately 20–30% of the population of Roman Italy were slaves.[3]

   2. The Greek word *doulos* is used 127 times in the New Testament in 119 verses. Clearly this was a cultural concept that was well understood.

   3. A bondservant was an individual bound to another in subjection or subserviency. It may be voluntary or involuntary. It described one who was in a permanent relation of servitude to another. It conveys the idea of the slave's close binding ties with their master—belonging to him, obligated to him, desiring to do his will in a committed relationship of servitude. In other words, the will of the *doulos* is consumed by the will of the master.

F. In their letters, the apostles introduced themselves as the *doulos* of Christ and of God. This identity is surprising and seems to stand in contrast to that of privileged sons of the Most High God.

---

[2] Trench, Richard Chenevix. *Synonyms of the New Testament*. Aeterna Press, 2015. Kindle Edition.
[3] Joshel, Sandra R. *Slavery in the Roman World*. New York: Cambridge University Press, 2010. Print

Paul, a <u>doulos</u> of Christ Jesus... (Romans 1:1); Paul and Timothy, <u>doulos</u> of Christ Jesus (Philippians 1:1); Epaphras, who is one of you and a <u>doulos</u> of Christ Jesus (Colossians 4:12); Paul, a <u>doulos</u> of God (Titus 1:1); James, a <u>doulos</u> of God and of the Lord Jesus Christ (James 1:1); Simon Peter, a <u>doulos</u> and apostle of Jesus Christ (2 Peter 1:1); Jude, a <u>doulos</u> of Jesus Christ (Jude 1)

G.   A *doulos* had no life of his own—no will of his own—no purpose of his own—no plan of his own. "All of him" was subject to the master. It is a picture of complete and total surrender of one person to another.

II.   EMBRACING THE IDENTITY OF A BONDSERVANT

A.   There is no doubt that in Greek and Roman culture the term *doulos* could be degrading, involuntary, and permanent. Paul and Peter, however, elevate the meaning to a Hebrew sense described in the Old Testament.

[12] "If your brother, a Hebrew man or a Hebrew woman, is sold to you, he shall serve you six years, and in the seventh year <u>you shall let him go free</u> from you. [13] And when you let him go free from you, you shall not let him go empty-handed. [14] You shall furnish him liberally out of your flock, out of your threshing floor, and out of your winepress. As the Lord your God has blessed you, you shall give to him. [15] You shall remember that you were a slave in the land of Egypt, and the Lord your God redeemed you; therefore I command you this today. [16] But if he says to you, '<u>I will not go out from you</u>,' <u>because he loves you and your household</u>, since he is well-off with you, [17] then you shall take an awl, and put it through his ear into the door, and he shall be your slave forever. And to your female slave you shall do the same. (Deuteronomy 15:12-17 ESV)

[2] When you buy a Hebrew slave, he shall serve six years, and in the seventh <u>he shall go out free</u>, for nothing. [3] If he comes in single, he shall go out single; if he comes in married, then his wife shall go out with him. [4] If his master gives him a wife and she bears him sons or daughters, the wife and her children shall be her master's, and he shall go out alone. [5] But if the slave plainly says, '<u>I love my master</u>, my wife, and my children; <u>I will not go out free</u>,' [6] then his master shall bring him to God [bring him to the judges- NIV], and he shall bring him to the door or the doorpost. And his master shall bore his ear through with an awl, and he shall be his slave forever. (Exodus 21:2-6 ESV)

B.   In this sense, the apostles were saying, "I am a man who has made a choice. I'm staying in this Master's house because I love Him!"

C.   The piercing of the slave's ear with an awl was done in the site of judges to ensure that the decision was completely voluntary. Such a decision could not be forced.

D. This choice—this identity—comes into clearer focus when we now consider the words of the Apostle John.

¹ The revelation of Jesus Christ, which God gave him <u>to show to his servants</u> [doulos] the things that must soon take place. He made it known by sending his angel to his servant [doulos] John, ² who bore witness to the word of God and to the testimony of Jesus Christ, even to all that he saw. (Revelation 1:1-2 ESV)

E. Let us consider the prophetic promise released on the day of Pentecost when Peter quoted the prophet Joel.

¹⁷ And in the last days it shall be, God declares, that I will pour out my Spirit on all flesh, and your sons and your daughters shall prophesy, and your young men shall see visions, and your old men shall dream dreams; ¹⁸ even on <u>my male servants</u> [doulos] <u>and female servants</u> [doule] in those days I will pour out my Spirit, and they shall prophesy. (Acts 2:17-18 ESV)

F. The point being: revelation is for the bondservants!

G. Do you want to occasionally put your ear near the Lord's door, hoping to hear a little prophetic tidbit? Be careful what you do with your itching ears. When you put your ear near the Lord's door, He comes at you with an awl.

III. GOD'S CALL TO THE BONDSERVANT TO LIVE IN HIS HOUSE

A. It's important to note that from God's perspective slavery was never meant to be permanent. His design for the Hebrews handling of servants reflects his ultimate desire to set people free.

For freedom Christ has set us free; stand firm therefore, and do not submit again to a yoke of slavery. (Galatians 5:1 ESV)

B. The willing bondservant entered into a special destiny with the master. In the Hebrew understanding, he would become as one of the family and be entrusted with great responsibility for his master's business.

C. A *doulos* is not a hired servant who serves because it is their job. That word represents the servant in his activity for *the work*, not in his relation to *a person*.[4] It does not carry the same permanence and weight as that of a *doulos*.

D. Many times we see our service to God as *optional* or *occasional* because we view it as *something we do* instead of *who we are*.

---

[4] Trench.

E.   The awl being driven into the doorpost of the master's house was a clear message. It meant that this person was not going anywhere. They were permanently connected to that house and that master. They could never go free again; but the wonderful news was they could never be sold again either.

F.   When the hole in the ear was healed, traditionally a gold earring was placed in it to signify the master's great value for the servant's voluntary love.

G.   A spiritual bondservant lifestyle leads to true freedom from ungodliness, as our heavenly Master delivers us from the bondage and servitude of sin. We literally have been purchased with a price from one master and delivered unto another.

H.   The spiritual bondservant of Christ understands that a price has literally been paid in order to redeem them. This transaction carries with it a requirement to leave behind the ways of the former master and come under the new ways of his master's house.

No servant can serve two masters, for either he will hate the one and love the other, or he will be devoted to the one and despise the other. You cannot serve God and money [Greek: mamonas]." (Luke 16:13 ESV)

1.   Mamonas- Mammon, treasure, riches (where it is personified and opposed to God).

2.   A Chaldee or Syriac word meaning "wealth" or "riches" (Luke 16:9-11); also, by personification, the god of riches (Matthew 6:24; Luke 16:9-11).[5]

[18] Flee from sexual immorality. Every other sin a person commits is outside the body, but the sexually immoral person sins against his own body. [19] Or do you not know that your body is a temple of the Holy Spirit within you, whom you have from God? You are not your own, [20] for you were bought with a price. So glorify God in your body. (1 Corinthians 6:18-20 ESV)

...the church of God, which he obtained with his own blood. (Acts 20:28 ESV)

And they sang a new song, saying, "Worthy are you to take the scroll and to open its seals, for you were slain, and by your blood you ransomed people for God from every tribe and language and people and nation... (Revelation 5:9 ESV)

[11] For the grace of God has appeared, bringing salvation for all people, [12] training

---

[5] "Mammon - Easton's Bible Dictionary." *Blue Letter Bible*. Web. 26 May 2016.

us to renounce ungodliness and worldly passions, and to live self-controlled, upright, and godly lives in the present age, ¹³ waiting for our blessed hope, the appearing of the glory of our great God and Savior Jesus Christ, ¹⁴ who gave himself for us <u>to redeem us</u> from all lawlessness and to purify for himself a people for his own possession who are zealous for good works. (Titus 2:11-14 ESV)

Christ <u>redeemed us</u> from the curse of the law by becoming a curse for us—for it is written, "Cursed is everyone who is hanged on a tree" (Galatians 3:13 ESV)

¹⁸ knowing that <u>you were ransomed</u> from the futile ways inherited from your forefathers, not with perishable things such as silver or gold, ¹⁹ but with the precious blood of Christ, like that of a lamb without blemish or spot. (1 Peter 1:18-19 ESV)

<u>But you are</u> a chosen race, a royal priesthood, a holy nation, <u>a people for his own possession</u>, that you may proclaim the excellencies of him who called you out of darkness into his marvelous light. (1 Peter 2:9 ESV)

Live as people who are free, not using your freedom as a cover-up for evil, but living as servants [doulos] of God. (1 Peter 2:16 ESV)

IV.   IT IS GOOD IN THE MASTER'S HOUSE

A.   Two big recurring hindrances arise for believers that prevent them from moving forward in their spiritual lives.

1.   Many say, "I have no idea what God wants from me."

2.   Most say, "I don't think I have what I need to accomplish what God's asking me to do."

B.   Firstly, we must understand that the master is responsible for his slave's duties. It is not the slave's responsibility to create his own tasks.

1.   We can rest assured that there is a master builder in this house who knows precisely how to fitly join all the pieces together according to His blueprint. We simply must be obedient to do what he tells us to do.

2.   It is vital that you don't measure your calling against another person's calling, and don't try to measure the success of your God-given assignments with someone else's man-made criteria.

C.   Secondly, we must understand that the master is responsible for providing for his slave's needs.

[25] "Therefore I tell you, do not be anxious about your life, what you will eat or what you will drink, nor about your body, what you will put on... [26] Look at the birds of the air: they neither sow nor reap nor gather into barns, and yet your heavenly Father feeds them. Are you not of more value than they?... [28] And why are you anxious about clothing? Consider the lilies of the field, how they grow: they neither toil nor spin,... [30] But if God so clothes the grass of the field,... will he not much more clothe you, O you of little faith? [31] Therefore do not be anxious, saying, 'What shall we eat?' or 'What shall we drink?' or 'What shall we wear?'... your heavenly Father knows that you need them all. [33] But seek first the kingdom of God and his righteousness, and all these things will be added to you. (Matthew 6:25-33 ESV)

D.   Think of the freedom and peace of mind that would come from the confidence of knowing that you have a Master who accepts responsibility for the needs of you, your family, your mission—all your needs.

E.   With this perspective, you can now better understand the Apostle Paul when he said, "I have learned the secret..."

[11] Not that I am speaking of being in need, for I have learned in whatever situation I am to be content. [12] I know how to be brought low, and I know how to abound. In any and every circumstance, I have learned the secret of facing plenty and hunger, abundance and need. [13] I can do all things through him who strengthens me... [19] And my God will supply every need of yours according to his riches in glory in Christ Jesus. (Philippians 4:10-13, 19 ESV)

F.   A person who is willing to bow is a person whom God can use. We must bow our hearts and joyously yield ourselves saying, "God, I just want what you want. My life is yours."

G.   It is the Lord's good pleasure to give each of us the desires of our heart. In time, we discover that the desires of His heart have actually become the desires of our own heart.

[3] Trust in the Lord, and do good; dwell in the land and befriend faithfulness. [4] Delight yourself in the Lord, and he will give you the desires of your heart. (Psalm 37:3-4 ESV)

H.   To embrace the identity of a *doulos* is the signature of maturity.

V.   BECOMING A BONDSERVANT OF THE HEART

A.   The Master says to you, "You are free to go." Will you leave?

⁶⁶ After this many of his disciples turned back and no longer walked with him. ⁶⁷ So Jesus said to the Twelve, "Do you want to go away as well?" ⁶⁸ Simon Peter answered him, "Lord, <u>to whom shall we go</u>? You have the words of eternal life, ⁶⁹ and we have believed, and have come to know, that you are the Holy One of God." (John 6:66-69 ESV)

B.   There must be a cry that erupts from our hearts that says, "It is better in Your house than anywhere else!"

Oh, taste and see that <u>the Lord is good! Blessed is the man</u> who takes refuge in him! (Psalm 34:8 ESV)

C.   God gives you dignity and honor. What did the world ever do for you?

D.   We must enter into the reality of Deuteronomy 15.

¹⁶ But if he says to you, 'I will not go out from you,' because <u>he loves you and your household</u>, since he is well-off with you, ¹⁷ then you shall take an awl, and put it through his ear into the door, and he shall be your slave forever. And to your female slave you shall do the same. (Deuteronomy 15:16-17 ESV)

E.   Christ is the model for the willing bondservant who chooses out of love.

In sacrifice and offering you have not delighted, but you have given me an open [Hebrew: karah- to dig, pierce⁶] ear. (Psalm 40:6 ESV)

No one takes it from me, but I lay it down of my own accord. I have authority to lay it down, and I have authority to take it up again. <u>This charge I have received from my Father.</u>" (John 10:18 ESV)

F.   The ear that is pierced is the ear that hears the will of the Master.

¹⁹ So Jesus said to them, "Truly, truly, I say to you, the Son can do nothing of his own accord, but <u>only what he sees</u> the Father doing. For whatever the Father does, that the Son does likewise... ³⁰ "<u>I can do nothing on my own.</u> As I hear, I judge, and my judgment is just, because I seek <u>not my own will but the will of him who sent me.</u> (John 5:19, 30 ESV)

G.   This must be repeated again and again: *"It's all about intimacy."* Becoming submissive to another's will loses all negative meaning when it is born out of

---

⁶ "Lexicon: Strong's H3738 - Karah." *Blue Letter Bible.* Web. 24 June 2016.

love. Our choice to bind ourselves to the Lord's house is a choice made out of love and devotion to Him.

VI.   SERVANT SONS

A.   The parable of the prodigal son captures the essence of the Lord's call for both sonship and bondservants—*it is a tale of two sons.*

The Parable of the Prodigal Son (Luke 15:11-32)

B.   The privileged son squandered his provision on prostitutes. It was in the pig pen that he realizes that it was better in his Father's house. At the low point of his lusts and passions, he did not really resemble a son. The young prodigal is stunned, though, that—to his father—his identity as a son never ceased. His father's open arms and overwhelming value of him sealed a love in him, forever marking him as a *willing servant son.*

C.   We are all prodigals in various states of return. Most of us reach the pig pen; begin a journey back to the Father's house; stop, go back to the pig pen; begin to return in brokenness, go back to the pig pen again, etc. The Father continues to meet us on the road with a ring and robe, searching for the one who is lost.

D.   The elder brother lacked a revelation of the love of his father. He viewed his service to him as a thing of scorn rather than something that was a manifestation of an overwhelming love for his father, his father's house, and his father's family.

²⁸ The older brother became angry and <u>refused to go in</u>. So his father went out and pleaded with him. ²⁹ But he answered his father, 'Look! All these years <u>I've been slaving for you</u>... (Luke 15:28-29 NIV)

E.   This lack of revelation prevented him from experiencing the fullness of his father's goodness.

SECTION 2

Progressing in Consecration and a Fasted Lifestyle

"When exercised with a pure heart and a right motive, fasting may provide us with a key to unlock doors where other keys have failed; a window opening up new horizons in the unseen world; a spiritual weapon of God's providing, 'mighty, to the pulling down of strongholds.'"

Arthur Wallis

Nazirite Consecration

During flashpoint moments of human history, God fashioned an unprecedented strategy to confront the spiritual wanderings of nations and God's people. The strategies of man were not strong enough to turn the tide of demonic rebellion or spiritual complacency that was emerging. Thus, God's divine strategy was not an instructional plan, but his Spirit moving through consecrated people—God called them Nazirites or "separated ones".

Nazirite consecration is often one of the most misunderstood, misrepresented and marginalized ministries. Yet, it is a ministry that finds its inception in God's heart; it blazes across the pages of Scripture's darkest hours.

At the end of the age, God is now raising up consecrated prophetic voices to respond to His heart preceding the Lord's return. What are you going to do when your response becomes the hinge of history through which God moves?

I.   **HINGES OF HISTORY**

    A.   Human history is an unfolding of transitional generations. At these critical junctures of history, these unprecedented transitional moments, doors for great blessing or judgment swing wide open. History hinges on the response of God's people in those "spiritual vacuums." Often, it is a matter of life and death. It is a matter of responding to the movements of God's heart.

        "He who has an ear, let him hear what the Spirit says to the churches." (Revelation 2:29 ESV)

        "Take care then how you hear, for to the one who has, more will be given, and from the one who has not, even what he thinks that he has will be taken away." (Luke 8:18 ESV)

    B.   Jesus warned His listeners to actively prepare their hearts to hear, understanding their responsibility as "hearers" to discern and rightly respond to the word of the Lord during these hinges of history.

    C.   Nazirites would emerge during these hinges of history. These Nazirites were consecrated prophetic voices whose *message* and *lifestyles* would expose the spiritual bankruptcy of their generation and call them back to repentance and renewed covenant with God. Accordingly, God would raise up Nazirites before transitional generations where He was about to move in an unique way.

    D.   Nazirites are ordinary people who live in an extraordinary way. There are many biblical examples of Nazirites throughout Scripture: Samson, Samuel,

Elijah, and John the Baptist to name a few.

II.   **CALLED TO NAZIRITE CONSECRATION**

A.   The Nazirite vow is God's response to a longing in His people. God is the One who initiates this ministry in the earth.

¹ And the Lord spoke to Moses, saying, ² "Speak to the people of Israel and say to them, <u>When either a man or a woman makes a special vow, the vow of a Nazirite</u>, to separate himself to the Lord... (Numbers 6:1-2 ESV)

¹¹ And <u>I raised up</u> some of your sons for prophets, and <u>some of your young men for Nazirites</u>. Is it not indeed so, O people of Israel?" declares the Lord. ¹² "But you made the Nazirites drink wine, and commanded the prophets, saying, 'You shall not prophesy.' (Amos 2:11-12 ESV)

B.   In the early 1900's, Rees Howells (founder of the Bible College of Wales) was a man whom God called to Nazirite consecration. In response to this invitation from the Lord, Howells was reluctant at first. He had never seen this calling modeled in real life, though it was demonstrated throughout Scripture.

I told the Lord it would be far better to die than to do this. I was just thirty years old... I told the Holy Spirit I knew of no one who had been called to such a thing in this generation—how could I ever give in to it?¹ –Rees Howells

C.   The Spirit moved through Rees Howells' Nazirite consecration:

... if at the beginning the world was affecting [Rees], by the end it was he who was affecting the world, for people sensed the presence of God with him, and said so. Even some with no religious faith would take their hats off when they passed him in the streets; and one old man used to tell people, "You mark my words: there goes a modern John the Baptist." An evidence of the effect he had on the district was seen later. When a man, who did not know his name, simply asked the ticket collector at the station where "the man with the Holy Ghost" lived, and was directed to Mr. Howells.² -Norman Grubb

D.   Nazirite consecration gives voice to wholeheartedness. It is a picture of a people who are fiercely intentional to pursue wholehearted love unto God.

1.   Consecration- (Numbers 6:2) Nazirites pursued holiness in a radical way, amidst much unholiness and idolatry (Numbers 6:2). It was a prophetic image of the laying down of one's life as a "living sacrifice" to follow the

¹ Grubb, Norman. *Rees Howells: Intercessor.* Fort Washington: Christian Literature Crusade, 1952. Print.
² Grubb.

beautiful and glorious One, Jesus. (Romans 12:1-2).

"Blessed are those who hunger and thirst for righteousness, for they shall be satisfied." (Matthew 5:6 ESV)

2. Separation- (Numbers 6:3-4) by abstaining from wine, grapes, and the skin of grapes, they refrained from even legitimate pleasures in exchange for pursuing the ultimate pleasures of loving God – (Numbers 6:3-4; Song of Songs 1:2).

   a. Nazirites live fasted lifestyles in search of the the best "wine" – the wine of the Spirit!

   b. Nazirites are pleasure seekers in pursuit of the supreme pleasures of loving God and being loved by God.

      And do not be drunk with wine, in which is dissipation; but be filled with the Spirit... (Ephesians 5:18 NKJV)

      ...in your presence there is fullness of joy; at your right hand are pleasures forevermore. (Psalm 16:11 ESV)

      They feast on the abundance of your house, and you give them drink from the river of your delights. (Psalm 36:8 ESV)

3. Dedication- (Numbers 6:5) Long hair was a symbol of their strength and dedication to God. You could tell ones dedication by the length of their hair. This was a public mark of consecration and open accountability.

   a. When a Nazirite broke their covenant, they had to repent, shave their head, and renew their vow. However, they were not disqualified. (Numbers 6:9)

   b. Nazirites run to God in love and repentance, rather than away from Him in shame. The bondage of shame accuses the atoning blood of Christ of being like just another "fig leaf."

4. Purity- (Numbers 6:7) staying clear of dead bodies was a symbol of radically turning from things that defile and pursuing righteousness and holiness at all costs. This was a symbol of their commitment to the highest degree of purity and holiness.

"Blessed are the pure in heart, for they shall see God." (Matthew 5:8 ESV)

5. "Whatever else"- (Numbers 6:21): The Nazirite vow was just the starting point of consecration in the Lord's heart. Nazirites are not concerned with how little they can get by on in their relationship with God, but how far they can go in love.

"This is the law of the Nazirite. <u>But if he vows an offering to the Lord above his Nazirite vow</u>, as he can afford, in exact accordance with the vow that he takes, then he shall do in addition to the law of the Nazirite." (Numbers 6:21)

E. Nazirite consecration was an invitation to everyone, not just a specific group of people. While there were limitations on the Jewish priesthood, the Nazirite vow was an invitation for anyone to make a deep commitment to God.

F. Though often misunderstood, the Nazirite vow is birthed out of prophetic inspiration in God, rather than legalism or our outward appearance or actions. It is the Holy Spirit and the grace of God which empowers us to pursue Him.

For the <u>grace of God</u> has appeared, bringing salvation for all people, training us to <u>renounce ungodliness</u> and <u>worldly passions</u>, and to live self-controlled, upright, and godly lives in the present age... (Titus 2:11-12 ESV)

G. Nazirites don't apologize for their zeal for Jesus. They let their character speak for itself.

III. THE SPIRITUAL LANDSCAPE OF NAZIRITES

A. Many times throughout Scripture, when the nation of Israel was in deep moral decline, compromise, spiritual wandering and living abandoned from the law of God. God would raise up a unique company of individuals that He called Nazirites. God would use these consecrated ones, or "set apart ones," to call a nation back to the intents of His heart.

B. It is true that in every generation, God desires His people to be blameless and holy. However, in transitional generations the necessity for consecration and holiness increases. We cannot make a difference unless we are actually different.

C. We cannot earn God's love, but we can posture our spirits to experience more of it.

"...He chose us in Him before the foundation of the world, that we should be holy and blameless before him." (Ephesians 1:4 ESV)

D.   God is restoring biblical prophetic voices on the moorings of humility, integrity, and character. Man doesn't define a prophetic voice, God does.

IV.   CONSECRATED ONES

A.   Regarding the Nazirite Vow, Charles Spurgeon said:

> *Taking your place before the Cross of Christ, as a self-judged sinner, and resting your soul in faith on him who died there, you become a believer, a saved man; but it is not until you learn the power of that cross upon your spirit to deliver you from the attractions of the world—in short, to crucify you to the world, and the world to you—that you become a thorough disciple, or a truly separated one.*[3] *–Charles Spurgeon*

B.   Consecration, in the spirit of a Nazirite, is a *voluntary response* to the heart of God burning in jealous love. It was an Old Testament depiction of the New Testament call to the First Commandment lifestyle—an *invitation* to love God at the fullest level in *response* to the burning eyes of Jesus the Bridegroom.

C.   Consecration is the fruit of revelation. If we have not touched the love of God we cannot love Him in return. Nazirites respond to the claim of God on their lives.

> *¹⁹ Or do you not know that your body is a temple of the Holy Spirit within you, whom you have from God? You are not your own, ²⁰ for you were bought with a price. So glorify God in your body. (1 Corinthians 6:19-20 ESV)*

> *¹⁴ As obedient children, do not be conformed to the passions of your former ignorance, ¹⁵ but as he who called you is holy, you also be holy in all your conduct, ¹⁶ since it is written, "You shall be holy, for I am holy." ... ¹⁸ knowing that you were ransomed from the futile ways inherited from your forefathers, not with perishable things such as silver or gold, ¹⁹ but with the precious blood of Christ, like that of a lamb without blemish or spot. (1 Peter 1:14-16, 18-19 ESV)*

> *For those whom he foreknew he also predestined to be conformed to the image of his Son, in order that he might be the firstborn among many brothers. (Romans 8:29 ESV)*

V.   JOHN THE BAPTIST'S EXAMPLE

A.   John the baptist is a New Testament example of Nazirite consecration. In Matthew 11, Jesus actually vindicated John's *lifestyle*, *message*, and *consecration*

---

[3] Spurgeon, Charles. *The Sword and the Trowel*. London: Nabu, 2010. Print.

before all of Israel.

1. "He will be great"- In the womb, John was marked for greatness in the eyes of the Lord. John the baptist's lifestyle got him the evaluation from Jesus of being "the greatest man ever born of a woman." (Matthew 11:11). Greatness is ultimately defined by the age to come. John lived under the shadow of the definition of greatness in the age to come.

2. "He will not drink wine"- In transitional hours of human history, the call to consecration increases. You can only make a difference if you're actually different. The garden of the heart must be guarded.

3. "He will turn the hearts of many"- God would use Nazirites to release divine influence to turn the hearts of many. John was called to the ministry of turning human hearts.

4. "He will go before Him in the spirit and power of Elijah"- It is interesting to note that John walked in the spirit and power of Elijah without ever doing a sign and a wonder.

B. What was needed to pierce through the shroud of 400 years of prophetic silence?

...the word of God came to John the son of Zechariah in the wilderness. (Luke 3:2 ESV)

C. The spirit of prophecy is the declaration of the Word of the Lord—under the anointing of the Spirit—that polarizes the nation, tenderizes the heart, and brings men to repentance by removing the "gray area" where human hearts think they are safe to remain neutral. The Word of the Lord changes history. The Word of the Lord divides things. Information alone does not change the heart. The Spirit of God changes the heart.

VI. NAZIRITES AT THE END OF THE AGE

A. The promise at the end of the age is that God will once again send the spirit of Elijah to turn the hearts of multitudes for the sake of preparing the way for the Second Coming of Christ. The raising up of spiritual patriarchs and matriarchs, mothers and fathers, gave birth to Nazirite spiritual sons and daughters through prayer. Spirit begets spirit.

"Behold, I will send you Elijah the prophet before the great and awesome day of the Lord comes. [6] And he will turn the hearts of fathers to their children and the hearts of children to their fathers, lest I come and strike the land with a decree

of utter destruction." (Malachi 4:5-6 ESV)

B.   The primary spearheads of the move of God before the first coming of Jesus the Messiah were a group of praying, worshiping, evangelizing, prophetic old people gripped by the Spirit of God for what He was about to do in the coming generation. On the tail end of 400 years of prophetic silence, before John the baptist's birth, we see the wind of the Spirit moving upon fathers and mothers of the faith:

1.   Zechariah and Elizabeth were contending for the promise of prophetic sons and daughters which had been delayed for many years, though scripture declares that they walked in righteousness before the LORD. They were parents who got severely apprehended by the Lord with a cry—not only for children, but for children who would walk in the ways of the Lord with a prophetic spirit.

2.   Anna, in Luke 2:36-38, fasted and prayed in the Temple, day and night, for decades preparing the way before Jesus' First Coming and standing as one of the first evangelists in the New Testament. She was widowed as a teen. Struck by the pain of losing her husband, she was faced with a choice: either she could turn in bitterness and offense, or she could throw herself into the heart of the LORD, her true husband, and became pained with longing for the manifestation of the promise of His coming.

3.   Simeon, in Luke 2:25-35, was a righteous and devout man who waited in prayer for many years for *"the consolation of Israel"* as he was instructed by Holy Spirit that he would not see death until he had seen the Lord's Christ.

C.   Oh, that our hearts may never grow comfortable with the pain of delay and the nagging ache of unfulfilled promises in a generation!

D.   God has a unique call to prepare and Nazirites actually become an embodiment of what God was speaking, doing, and requiring of the generation that would soon find the transition upon them. To be a voice requires a lifestyle.

E.   A dire need in this generation is for the Word of the Lord, not just the delivery of information. The Lord is going to release the spirit of prophecy. The word of God that has been feasted on for many decades will become the Word of the Lord over time. Nazirites at the end of the age are forged in the wilderness, where they go deep in the word of God for the sake of what is coming in the future.

VII. REFUSE TO BE A PUBLIC SUCCESS AND A PRIVATE FAILURE

The danger of Nazirite consecration is to be holy on the outside, but inwardly carry a hard and self-righteous heart that hides behind the mask of righteousness and impressive outward actions that disguise a bankrupt soul. Only the fire of inward intimacy, the filling of the Holy Spirit along with continuously receiving God's mercy and delight for us, even when we fail, can deliver us from the Pharisaical heart.

Nazirites who are not living with intimacy with the Lord also face the danger of self-righteousness when they rejoice in their commitment to the Lord Jesus and not in Jesus Himself. Just like the Pharisee who despised the tax collector, in Luke 18:9, we will admire our own dedication while looking down on that of others. Too often we judge others by their actions, while judging ourselves by our intentions. The heart of those who rejoice in their own strength will end up in one of two pitfalls: either arrogance or accomplishment...or self-hatred as an unworthy son. Only embracing the grace of God to us with humility can help us avoid this.

If the most important thing was a disciplined lifestyle, then surely the Pharisees would be our role models! They knew the scriptures better than anyone and they rigorously kept the law, yet their hearts were aloof toward God and toward people. Discipline neither has the power nor the ability to satisfy the human heart. The human heart is made alive by romance, intimacy, and mystery [with God] and is fueled by passion and adventure. If we substitute these with discipline we will end up with a hard, cold, wanting heart of a Pharisee. When discipline replaces the place of love and intimacy, the only time we will feel loved is when we think we are living up to God's standards. When we fail, we'll believe that we are no longer loved. The Consecration and discipline of the Nazirite must spring from the filling of the spirit and the fire of God's jealousy on the human heart.[4] –Mike Bickle

---

[4] Engle, Lou. *Nazirite DNA*. Pasadena: TheCall, 2015. Print.

Grace for Fasting: Hunger for God

Most Christians who are pursuing a wholehearted lifestyle wrestle with questions about fasting at some point. Usually, the questions are provoked by the weakness of our flesh and its natural response to hate fasting, but there are also important spiritual issues related to maturity and truth.

This study is meant to bring clarity and energize fasting as a vital part of your wholehearted pursuit of God.

I.   THERE HAVE ALWAYS BEEN QUESTIONS ABOUT FASTING. THE MOST PRESSING ONE OF ALL IS: "CAN WE STOP NOW?"

> *² The people of Bethel had sent Sharezer and Regem-Melek, together with their men, to entreat the Lord ³ by asking the priests of the house of the Lord Almighty and the prophets, "Should I mourn and fast in the fifth month, as I have done for so many years?" (Zechariah 7:2-3 NIV)*

   A.   This pressing question was on the mind of not only everyone in Bethel, who had organized a delegation to seek an answer, but clearly it was the question of the entire nation. God's response was to "all the people" making it an issue of national importance.

> *⁴ Then the word of the Lord Almighty came to me: ⁵ "Ask <u>all the people of the land</u> and the priests, 'When you fasted...'" (Zechariah 7:4-5 NIV)*

   B.   The big question of Zechariah 7 was, "Can we stop fasting in the fifth month?"

   C.   Historical context- There was only one fast, Yom Kippur (Day of Atonement), required in the Law of Moses. Trauma and tradition had added an additional four fasts during the exile in Babylon. All of these fasts were connected to specific tragic events related to the destruction of Jerusalem and Solomon's temple in 586 BC.

      1.   Fast in the fourth month- Babylon's army breached Jerusalem's walls on the ninth day of the fourth month (2 Kings 25:3-4; Jeremiah 39:2).

      2.   Fast in the fifth month- The Temple in Jerusalem was burned (2 Kings 25:8-9). The most tragic day for Israel is the day the Temple was destroyed. According to the Talmud, on the very same day, the ninth day of the fifth month of Av (August), Solomon's temple was destroyed by the Babylonians in 586 BC, and Herod's temple (Zerubbabel's) by the Romans in 70 AD.

3. Fast in the seventh month- This was to commemorate the assassination of Gedaliah (2 Kings 25:25; Jeremiah 41:2). Nebuchadnezzar made Gedaliah governor of Judah (2 Kings 25:22-25). Gedaliah respected and cared for Jeremiah (Jeremiah 39:11-14; 40:5) just as his father had done. He only reigned for two months, before Jewish zealots led by Ishmael killed him.

4. Fast in the tenth month- This marked the beginning of the siege of the city of Jerusalem (2 Kings 25:1).

D. After 70 years of fasting while in Babylonian exile, the people thought it was inappropriate to continue with the fast since their return to Jerusalem marked a great victory for God's people. Essentially they were asking, "Isn't now the time for *celebration*?"

E. God did not answer their question in the way they expected. These delegates wanted a simple yes or no answer, when in reality they already knew which answer they sought.

F. Many times our attitude can be summed up like this: "God, just tell me what you want me to do, and I'll do it." The fact is we would not. The Lord knows our faith must be founded on something stronger than just rules and regulations. He knows it must be grounded in an encounter with him.

II.   ARE YOU ASKING THE WRONG QUESTION?

A. God's response took an unexpected turn when he answered their question with a question.

"Say to all the people of the land and the priests, When you fasted and mourned in the fifth month and in the seventh, for these seventy years, <u>was it for me that you fasted?</u>" (Zechariah 7:5 ESV)

B. Notice that God knew they were really asking about all of the fasts—not just the one in the fifth month. It was a subtle trick question to end all of the fasts.

C. This was a stunning question that caught everyone off guard. In a moment, God exposed that the fasts they were observing had the wrong focus. They had been fasting because of everything they had lost, but God asked if they had even thought about Him in the process.

D. God went further with his questioning by also connecting the problem with their feasts.

And when you eat and when you drink, do you not eat for yourselves and drink for yourselves [feasting- NIV]? (Zechariah 7:6 ESV)

E.   God not only exposed the misplaced focus of seventy years of fasting, but he also highlighted the same error in their feasting. That wasn't even a question on their minds, but the same spirit of error and self-centeredness has infected both their fasts *and* their feasts. God didn't ask *what* were you fasting and feasting for? He asked *who* were you fasting and feasting for?

F.   His redirection of the question turned the issue of fasting and feasting to matters of the heart.

G.   He exposed that by asking the wrong question it would lead them down the same path as their fathers who had gone into exile. After only a few short years back in Jerusalem, they were already heading down the same path. Essentially God was saying, "Look where it got them."

⁷ Were not these the words that the Lord proclaimed by the former prophets, when Jerusalem was inhabited and prosperous, with her cities around her, and the South and the lowland were inhabited?"… ¹¹ But they refused to pay attention and turned a stubborn shoulder and stopped their ears that they might not hear. ¹² They made their hearts diamond-hard lest they should hear the law and the words that the Lord of hosts had sent by his Spirit through the former prophets. (Zechariah 7:7, 11-12 ESV)

III.   WHO ARE YOU FASTING FOR?

A.   The storyline of Zechariah 7-8 highlights that God is looking for people to encounter Him in times of both peace *and* trouble—times of both celebration *and* mourning.

B.   The fasting of the people in exile was based solely on their self-centeredness and what they had lost. In their mourning, the only thing they were focused on was themselves. The height of their mourning did not go beyond grieving over the pain and loss of their carnal desires.

C.   Likewise the same was true of their feasts. While they were treating the feasts as opportunity for celebration, still they were only focused on themselves. Both the issues of eating and not eating are about having our hearts postured toward an encounter with God.

IV.   WHILE THE CHURCH TODAY IS EXPERIENCING A RESURGENCE OF INTEREST IN FASTING, THERE IS ALSO A GROWING CRITICISM. WHAT ARE WE TO THINK?

A. There are some New Testament warnings in the epistles that commonly get used as arguments against fasting. However, these are mainly about distortions in teaching and not against fasting altogether. These are weak arguments taken out of context.

> [1] *Now the Spirit expressly says that in later times some will <u>depart from the faith</u> by devoting themselves to <u>deceitful spirits and teachings of demons</u>, [2] through the insincerity of <u>liars</u> whose consciences are seared, [3] who forbid marriage and <u>require abstinence from foods that God created to be received with thanksgiving by those who believe and know the truth</u>. [4] For everything created by God is good, and <u>nothing is to be rejected</u> if it is received with thanksgiving (1 Timothy 4:1-4 ESV)*

> [20] *If with Christ you died to the elemental spirits of the world, <u>why, as if you were still alive in the world, do you submit to regulations</u>— [21] "Do not handle, <u>Do not taste</u>, Do not touch" [22] (referring to things that all perish as they are used)—according to human precepts and teachings? [23] These have indeed an appearance of wisdom in promoting self-made religion and asceticism and <u>severity to the body</u>, but they are of no value in stopping the indulgence of the flesh. (Colossians 2:20-23 ESV)*

> *<u>"All things are lawful,"</u> but not all things are helpful. "All things are lawful," but not all things build up. (1 Corinthians 10:23 ESV)*

B. The more damaging argument that is experiencing a growth in popularity involves the issue of God's grace in the life of the believer. There are two main criticisms of fasting based on a misunderstanding of God's grace.

   1. Doesn't the arrival of the kingdom in the ministry of Jesus make fasting obsolete? Isn't it like trying to put new wine in an old wineskin?

   2. Doesn't the finished work of the cross and ongoing presence of the Holy Spirit mean we should now celebrate?

C. The question of the Bethel delegates in Zechariah 7 mirrors the question being asked among some Christians today. "Isn't the need for fasting cancelled because of the victory we have received through grace? Shouldn't we just be celebrating because of all we have gained?" In a similar way, this is a "trojan horse" position with broader intentions and ramifications that only serve to reduce the level of our pursuit of God.

D. Indeed, the free gift of grace has made all things available to us. We cannot do anything to earn it. We cannot strive by any means to obtain it. All things are given to us through the free gift grace and the finished work of the cross.

> *³ Blessed be the God and Father of our Lord Jesus Christ, who has blessed us in Christ with <u>every spiritual blessing</u> in the heavenly places, ⁴ even as he chose us in him before the foundation of the world, that we should be holy and blameless before him. In love ⁵ he predestined us for adoption as sons through Jesus Christ, according to the purpose of his will, ⁶ to the praise of <u>his glorious grace</u>, with which he has blessed us in the Beloved. (Ephesians 1:3-6 ESV)*

E.   It would be a misunderstanding of grace to think that it takes the place of the need for spiritual hunger and wholehearted pursuit of God. Grace does not make fasting obsolete. Instead, grace super-charges it as a means of confronting compromise and spiritual apathy toward God in order to remove obstacles that hinder our relationship with him.

F.   The apostle Paul addressed the issue of food and mirrored the understanding given in Zechariah 7. Food cannot bring us closer to God.

> *<u>Food will not commend us to God</u>. We are no worse off if we do not eat, and no better off if we do. (1 Corinthians 8:8 ESV)*

> *³ Let not the one who eats despise the one who abstains, and let not the one who abstains pass judgment on the one who eats, for God has welcomed him. ⁴ Who are you to pass judgment on the servant of another? It is before his own master that he stands or falls. And he will be upheld, for the Lord is able to make him stand. ⁵ One person esteems one day as better than another, while another esteems all days alike. Each one should be fully convinced in his own mind. ⁶ The one who observes the day, observes it in honor of the Lord. <u>The one who eats, eats in honor of the Lord, since he gives thanks to God, while the one who abstains, abstains in honor of the Lord and gives thanks to God</u>. (Romans 14:3-6 ESV)*

G.   Grace highlights that having *the Giver* surpasses having the gifts. Grace enables us to love God with all of our heart, all of our soul, and all of our mind.

V.   WHAT DO YOU TRULY DESIRE?

A.   The debates about fasting are ultimately about our fundamental approach to spiritual hunger and maturity. We must believe that God is a rewarder of those who diligently seek him.

> *But without faith it is impossible to please Him, for he who comes to God must believe that He is, and that <u>He is a rewarder of those who diligently seek Him</u>. (Hebrews 11:6 NKJV)*

B.   The reward we are to seek in fasting is not first or mainly the gifts of God, but it is God himself.

C.   Fasting exposes the noise of our inner cravings and lusts that demand to be satisfied. In fasting, we are faced with the realities of our heart's true desires. Fasting gives us a way to make war on the deceitfulness of those desires. Subduing our carnal desires is not simply a matter of denial and discipline. Desire for God is required to endure this voluntary pain.

D.   In fasting, desire for the world loosens its grip on the affection of our hearts. We can join with the Apostle Paul and declare that we gladly will lose everything for the sake of gaining Christ.

Indeed, I count everything as loss because of the surpassing worth of knowing Christ Jesus my Lord. For his sake I have suffered the loss of all things and count them as rubbish, in order that I may gain Christ (Philippians 3:8 ESV)

E.   Let us resolve that both our feasting and our fasting will be about encountering God. Our celebrations are not just opportunities to disengage and check out. Likewise, our fastings cannot be wrongfully based on self-centered motives or efforts. Let's posture our hearts to acknowledge our need for greater spiritual hunger. We need more of Him!

Fasting expresses, rather than creates, hunger for God.[1] *–John Piper*

---

[1] Piper, John. *A Hunger for God: Desiring God through Fasting and Prayer.* Wheaton: Crossway, 1997. Print.

Grace for Fasting: Maranatha

What is to be the universal heart cry of all Christians?

> *⁷ And will not God give justice to his elect, <u>who cry to him day and night</u>? Will he delay long over them? ⁸ I tell you, he will give justice to them speedily. Nevertheless, <u>when the Son of Man comes, will he find faith on earth?</u>" (Luke 18:7-8 ESV)*

There is a heart cry that is directly connected to the return of Jesus Christ. The unending cry for justice in Luke 18 will lead us to the revelation that Jesus *is* justice. His glorious return to the earth, as King and Judge, will answer the cry of the hearts longing for him.

The final words of the Bible are the promise of Jesus, "Yes, I am coming soon," and the response of the church, "Amen. Come, Lord Jesus!" This is not a coincidence. This promise and response sums up the whole Bible.

Many Christians *neglect* to fast because they fail to see the benefit in their spiritual lives, while others *refuse* to fast because they see it as an old system of belief that has no place in the life of believer under the new covenant. This study will reveal that fasting is a historical and vital part of connecting Christians with the blessed hope of Christ's return (Titus 2:13).

I.   FASTING WAS AN IMPORTANT PART OF LIFE IN THE EARLY CHURCH

A.   Fasting is a part of nearly every religion on the earth. For Israel, fasting was instituted by God as a way to humble oneself, repent of personal and corporate sin, and as a means of consecration from ungodly, worldly influence. This begs the question: Is Christianity merely following the pattern of countless other religions? While fasting is not unique to Christianity, it is distinct.

B.   Jesus did not abolish the practice of fasting upon his first coming. In fact, he expected fasting by declaring, "when," *not if,* "you fast."

> *¹⁶ "And <u>when you fast</u>, do not look gloomy like the hypocrites, for they disfigure their faces that their fasting may be seen by others. Truly, I say to you, they have received their reward. ¹⁷ But <u>when you fast</u>, anoint your head and wash your face, ¹⁸ that your fasting may not be seen by others but by your Father who is in secret. And your Father who sees in secret will reward you. (Matthew 6:16-18 ESV)*

C.   Fasting was an important practice of the apostles in establishing the direction and leadership of the early church.

¹ Now there were in the church at Antioch prophets and teachers, Barnabas, Simeon who was called Niger, Lucius of Cyrene, Manaen a lifelong friend of Herod the tetrarch, and Saul. ² While they were <u>worshiping the Lord and fasting</u>, the Holy Spirit said, "Set apart for me Barnabas and Saul for the work to which I have called them." ³ Then after fasting and praying they laid their hands on them and sent them off. (Acts 13:1-3 ESV)

And when they had appointed elders for them in every church, <u>with prayer and fasting</u> they committed them to the Lord in whom they had believed. (Acts 14:23 ESV)

But in all things we commend ourselves as ministers of God: in much patience, in tribulations, in needs, in distresses, in stripes, in imprisonments, in tumults, in labors, in sleeplessness [watchings], <u>in fastings</u>... (2 Corinthians 6:4-5 NKJV)

Are they ministers of Christ?—I speak as a fool—I am more: in labors more abundant, in stripes above measure, in prisons more frequently, in deaths often... in weariness and toil, in sleeplessness often [watchings], in hunger and thirst, <u>in fastings often</u>, in cold and nakedness... (2 Corinthians 11:27 NKJV)

> *There is concern in the hearts of many for the recovery of apostolic power. But how can we recover apostolic power while neglecting apostolic practice?[1]*
> *–Arthur Wallis*

D.   Some have asked why the New Testament doesn't speak more of fasting if it was so important. History reveals that the early church universally embraced the practice of fasting.

> *And let not your fastings be with the hypocrites, for they fast on the second (Monday) and the fifth (Thursday) day of the week; but do ye keep your fast on the fourth (Wednesday) and on the preparation (the sixth- Friday) day. (Didache- Christian teaching manual dated mid to late 1st century)[2]*

E.   It is interesting that the early church was living with the expectation of Christ's return sooner rather than later—in fact, in their own lifetime. Fasting was universally embraced and directly connected with the hope and longing of Jesus' second coming. There are two generations in the history of the church in which a *majority* of Christians live with a belief that Jesus is returning soon— the first century generation and the current generation. Not surprisingly, the practice of fasting is currently experiencing resurgence among God's people.

---

[1] Wallis, Arthur. *God's Chosen Fast*. Fort Washington: CLC Publications, 1968. Kindle edition.
[2] Kirby, Peter. "The Didache or Teaching of the Apostles." *Early Christian Writings*. 2016. Web. 12 July 2016.

II. NEW TESTAMENT CHRISTIAN FASTING MUST BE CONNECTED TO THE PRESENT REALITY OF THE KINGDOM OF GOD

A. We no longer grieve over personal and corporate sins that are merely "passed over" for a time. We now have the full revelation of atonement through Jesus Christ. Our sins are no longer *passed over* or *covered*. They are completely *removed* as far as the east is from the west. Our once sin-stained garments can now be made white as snow.

But now the righteousness of God has been manifested apart from the law, although the Law and the Prophets bear witness to it—the righteousness of God through faith in Jesus Christ for all who believe. For there is no distinction: for all have sinned and fall short of the glory of God, and are justified by his grace as a gift, through the redemption that is in Christ Jesus, whom God put forward as a propitiation by his blood, to be received by faith. This was to show God's righteousness, because in his divine forbearance he had passed over former sins. It was to show his righteousness at the present time, so that he might be just and the justifier of the one who has faith in Jesus. (Romans 3:21-26 ESV)

B. Fasting is not made obsolete for the Christian. Instead, it reaches its highest form by connecting us to the present reality of the kingdom of God.

"The great, central, decisive act of salvation for us today is past, not future. And on the basis of that past work of the Bridegroom, nothing can ever be the same again. The Lamb is slain. The blood is shed. The punishment of our sins is executed. Death is defeated. The Spirit is sent. The wine is new. And the old fasting mindset is simply not adequate." [3] *–John Piper*

C. Fasting can be seen as the *future-oriented* counterpart to the *past-oriented* feast of the Lord's table. In communion, we remember what he has done, and all our faith rests on that finished work. Communion is truly a thanksgiving feast. In fasting, we look forward to the coming promises not yet fulfilled as we hunger for greater revelation and manifestation of him. The longed-for kingdom is both present *and* future.

[23] For I received from the Lord what I also delivered to you, that the Lord Jesus on the night when he was betrayed took bread, [24] and when he had given thanks, he broke it, and said, "This is my body which is for you. Do this in remembrance of me." [25] In the same way also he took the cup, after supper, saying, "This cup is the new covenant in my blood. Do this, as often as you drink it, in remembrance of me." 26 For as often as you eat this bread and drink the cup, you proclaim the Lord's death until he comes. (1 Corinthians 11:23-26 ESV)

---

[3] Piper, John. *A Hunger for God: Desiring God through Fasting and Prayer.* Wheaton: Crossway, 1997. Print.

D.   The most important scripture in the New Testament concerning fasting is Matthew 9:14-17. Jesus described "new fasting" as a new patch that cannot be put on an old garment and as new wine being put into a new wineskin. This new fasting was directly connected to the revelation of Jesus as our bridegroom.

⁴ Then the disciples of John came to him, saying, "Why do we and the Pharisees fast, but your disciples do not fast?" ¹⁵ And Jesus said to them, "Can the wedding guests mourn as long as the <u>bridegroom</u> is with them? The days will come when the <u>bridegroom</u> is taken away from them, and <u>then they will fast</u>. ¹⁶ No one puts a piece of unshrunk cloth on an old garment, for the patch tears away from the garment, and a worse tear is made. ¹⁷ Neither is <u>new wine</u> put into old wineskins. If it is, the skins burst and the wine is spilled and the skins are destroyed. But <u>new wine is put into fresh wineskins</u>, and so both are preserved." (Matthew 9:14-17 ESV)

E.   The only other time Jesus referred to himself as "bridegroom" was in reference to himself returning at the end of the age (Matthew 25:1-13). Clearly Jesus thinks of himself as being gone for more than just the time in between his arrest and resurrection.

F.   The present reality is that Jesus is currently away. Some refuse to acknowledge Jesus' absence as though it somehow violates their faith that he dwells within us and never leaves us. These same people commonly also hold a low view or complete disregard for fasting. However, scripture specifically describes the present age of the church in these terms.

The days will come when the bridegroom is <u>taken away from them</u>, and then they will fast. (Matthew 9:15 ESV)

⁴ But I have said these things to you, that when their hour comes you may remember that I told them to you. "I did not say these things to you from the beginning, because I was with you. ⁵ But now I am going to him who sent me, and none of you asks me, 'Where are you going?' ⁶ But because I have said these things to you, sorrow has filled your heart. ⁷ Nevertheless, I tell you the truth: it is to your advantage that <u>I go away</u>, for if I do not <u>go away</u>, the Helper will not come to you. But if <u>I go</u>, I will send him to you. (John 16:4-7 ESV)

Yes, we are of good courage, and we would rather be away from the body and <u>at home with the Lord</u>. (2 Corinthians 5:8 ESV)

²³ I am hard pressed between the two. My desire is to <u>depart and be with Christ</u>, for that is far better. ²⁴ But to remain in the flesh is more necessary on your account. (Philippians 1:23-24 ESV)

The church still awaits the midnight cry, 'Behold, the bridegroom! Come out to meet him' (Mt 25:6). It is this age of the church that is the period of the absent Bridegroom. It is this age of the church to which our Master referred when He said, 'Then they will fast.' The time is now![4] –Arthur Wallis

G. There is an ache and cry created by the reality that Jesus is both here and yet not fully here. This cry comes from a hunger for greater intimacy that can only be satisfied by his full return.

> *[1] "Let not your hearts be troubled. Believe in God; believe also in me. [2] In my Father's house are many rooms. If it were not so, would I have told you that I go to prepare a place for you? [3] And if I go and prepare a place for you, I will come again and will take you to myself, that where I am you may be also. [4] And you know the way to where I am going." (John 14:1-4 ESV)*

> *The almost universal absence of regular fasting for the Lord's return is a witness to our satisfaction with the presence of the world and the absence of the Lord. This is not the way it should be.[5] –John Piper*

> *It will be a fasting and praying church that will hear the thrilling cry, 'Behold, the Bridegroom!' Tears shall then be wiped away, and the fast be followed by the feast at the marriage supper of the Lamb.[6] –Arthur Wallis*

III. **FASTING RELEASES THE CRY, "OUR LORD, COME!"**

A. The cry of the early church was "Maranatha," which means, "Our Lord, come!"

> *If anyone has no love for the Lord, let him be accursed. Our Lord, come! [maranatha] (1 Corinthians 16:22 ESV)*

B. In the same way the Hebrew word "amen" was preserved without change in almost every language of the world, so too "maranatha" was preserved from it's original Aramaic. It was the universal cry of the early church.

C. Jesus taught his disciples to pray, "Your kingdom come, your will be done, on earth as it is in heaven" (Matthew 6:10). The maranatha cry mirrors the disciple's prayer for the kingdom to fully come. These two things are not merely peripheral concerns. They are central to the beliefs and culture of the body of Christ.

> *The Bridegroom left on a journey just before the wedding, and the Bride*

---

[4] Wallis.
[5] Piper.
[6] Wallis.

cannot act as if things are normal. If she loves him, she will ache for his return.[7] *–John Piper*

D. Being content with the current state of the world and its influence on our lives will result in a lack of fasting. We don't fast when we are satisfied. Feasting at the table of the world causes our spirit to become dull. Being full of the world will prevent us from realizing our lack of hunger for God and the absence of longing for our Bridegroom's return.

E. The Bridegroom fast helps end our affair with the world and causes our hearts to burn with desire for the one to whom we have been betrothed. Our only response can be, "Come quickly!" It turns our attention to eternal matters and our focus to the greater fulfillment that we have not yet experienced.

> *Fasting is the exclamation point at the end of "Maranatha, come, Lord Jesus!"*[8] *–John Piper*

F. Fasting is *not* intended by God to be something we hate. It is a gift meant to tenderize our hearts and bring great change in our lives. Fasting is *not* an expression of emptiness. We fast not because we haven't tasted his presence, but because we have and can't be satisfied until the final consummation of our faith—the blessed hope.

> **Oh, taste and see that the Lord is good! Blessed is the man who takes refuge in him! (Psalm 34:8 ESV)**

G. The true heart response of the one who has tasted the goodness of the Lord is, "I want more!"

H. Consider that Anna's life of worship, prayer and fasting was in response to only seeing a small Old Testament fraction of what New Testament believers know of Christ. Anna's life teaches us that those who look for and long for Christ's coming will see more than others see.

I. Refuse to live as though the promise of reward in Matthew 6 is untrue!

> **...so that it will not be obvious to others that you are fasting, but only to your Father, who is unseen; and your Father, who sees what is done in secret, will reward you. (Matthew 6:18 NIV)**

> **Now there is in store for me the crown of righteousness, which the Lord, the righteous Judge, will award to me on that day—and not only to me, but also to**

---

[7] Piper.
[8] Piper.

__all who have longed for his appearing.__ (2 Timothy 4:8 NIV)

> *The Holy Spirit's final emphasis before Jesus' Second Coming will be on the intimate relationship between Him and His Bride. John described the Church as being in deep unity with the Holy Spirit at that time, saying and doing what the Spirit is saying and doing. The Holy Spirit will have revealed the Church's core identity. Instead of being called the 'Church,' she will have completely assumed her identity as the 'Bride' and will be fully participating in the bridal longing for the Bridegroom to 'come,' to return.[9] –Mike Bickle*

J. The declarations of Jesus and the words of scripture concerning the end of the age and his second coming (the Day of the Lord) are not to be taken as empty promises. The heart that is disconnected from these realities is left to cope with nothing more than self-help strategies and concealed disappointment.

K. The heart that is connected and longing for him endures the test of time, runs with perseverance, dares to do great exploits and finishes well. And there WILL BE a generation on the earth that gets to usher in the return of Christ!

---

[9] Bickle, Mike, and Dana Candler. *The Rewards of Fasting: Experiencing the Power and Affections of God*. Kansas City: Forerunner, 2005. Print.

Grace for Fasting: Motives Matter

There is grace for the fasted lifestyle that leads us into a greater desire for God and the fullness of His kingdom, which will culminate in the return of Jesus our Bridegroom God. This grace energizes wholeheartedness in the private and corporate lives of the church.

The voluntary embrace of weakness becomes the doorway of experiencing God's power in our personal lives and to the world around us.

> *Our seasons of fasting and prayer at the tabernacle have been high days indeed; never has heaven's gate stood wider; never have our heats been nearer the central glory.[1] – Charles Spurgeon*

I. **FOUR OBSERVATIONS FROM ACTS 13:1-3**

> *[1] Now there were in the church at Antioch prophets and teachers, Barnabas, Simeon who was called Niger, Lucius of Cyrene, Manaen a lifelong friend of Herod the tetrarch, and Saul. [2] While they were <u>worshiping</u> the Lord and <u>fasting</u>, the Holy Spirit said, "Set apart for me Barnabas and Saul for the work to which I have called them." [3] Then after <u>fasting</u> and <u>praying</u> they laid their hands on them and sent them off. (Acts 13:1-3 ESV)*

A. Firstly, this fasting was after Christ's coming, death, resurrection and ascension. Clearly the apostles did not think the finished work of the cross and the ministry of the Holy Spirit made fasting obsolete.

> **The days will come when the bridegroom is taken away from them, and then they will fast. (Matthew 9:15 ESV)**

B. Secondly, this fasting was a corporate fast. Clearly the apostles did not take Jesus teaching on private fasting (Matthew 6:16-18) to mean that no one can know you are fasting.

> *The critical issue is not whether people know you are fasting but whether you want them to know so that you can bask in their admiration.[2] –John Piper*

C. Thirdly, this fasting proved to be an occasion for the Holy Spirit's special guidance and direction. Clearly there is a connection between worship, fasting, prayer, and the decisive leading of the Holy Spirit in the life of the believer unto the establishment of the church.

---

[1] Bounds, Edward M. *The Complete Works of E.M. Bounds on Prayer: Experience the Wonders of God Through Prayer*. Grand Rapids: Baker Books, 2004. Print.

[2] Piper, John. *A Hunger for God: Desiring God through Fasting and Prayer*. Wheaton: Crossway, 1997. Print.

D.   Fourthly, this fasting changed the course of history. Clearly God chose the practice of fasting—along with worship and prayer—to be the launching pad for world missions and the expansion of His kingdom on the earth.

> *It is almost impossible to overstate the historical importance of that moment in the history of the world. Before this word from the Holy Spirit, there seems to have been no organized mission of the church beyond the eastern seacoast of the Mediterranean. Before this, Paul had made no missionary journeys westward to Asia Minor, Greece, Rome, or Spain. Before this Paul had not written any of his letters, which were all a result of his missionary travels, which began here.[3] –John Piper*

II.   MOTIVES MATTER

A.   Fasting is to be a part of our normal Christian experience. We must take careful consideration of our hearts so that we can pursue right objectives and obtain God's intended rewards.

> ***"Beware of practicing your righteousness before other people <u>in order to be seen by them</u>, for then you will have no reward from your Father who is in heaven." (Matthew 6:1 ESV)***

B.   Jesus warned to not let your fasting be like the hypocrites.

> ***"And when you fast, do not look gloomy <u>like the hypocrites</u> [Greek: hypokrites], for they disfigure their faces that their fasting may be seen by others. Truly, I say to you, they have received their reward. But when you fast, anoint your head and wash your face, that your fasting may not be seen by others but by your Father who is in secret. And your Father who sees in secret will reward you. (Matthew 6:16-18 ESV)***

C.   Hypocrite is a familiar word to us all, and we associate it with someone who doesn't practice what they preach. It is the worst description you can ever be labeled with as a Christian. Who were "the hypocrites" in this passage that Jesus was referring to?

   1.   *Hypokrites* means actor.[4]

   2.   This Greek word refers to the costumed performers of the theater.

D.   Why would it be hypocritical to fast and then on the outside look like you're fasting? Wouldn't the outside match the inside? By definition, why would it not

---

[3] Piper.
[4] "Lexicon: Strong's G5273 - Hypokritēs." *Blue Letter Bible.* Web. 13 July 2016.

be hypocritical to fast and then pretend to not be fasting? The answer lies in the motives of the heart.

1. Jesus is warning about having a heart that is motivated by human admiration. Their apparent openness about fasting was deceptive of what was really in their heart. The reward that they truly sought was the praise of men.

2. To make matters worse, their deceptive desire for the praise of men is hidden with a pretense of love for God.

    The danger of hypocrisy is that it is so successful. It aims at the praise of men. And it succeeds. But that's all.[5] –John Piper

3. Jesus warned that no other reward remains for those seeking the praise of men.

E. The difference in fasting Jesus wants us to understand can be simplified like this: *Being seen fasting versus fasting to be seen.*

F. Fast to be seen by God! Fasting, as Jesus instructed, makes your life a landing strip for the eyes of God. And there is unmistakable reward for those who seek Him.

And your Father who sees in secret <u>will reward you</u>. (Matthew 6:18 ESV)

And without faith it is impossible to please him, for whoever would draw near to God must believe that he exists and that <u>he rewards those who seek him</u>. (Hebrews 11:6 ESV)

G. In Matthew 6, Jesus warned that our giving, our praying, and our fasting should not be done like the hypocrites. Right in the middle of this discussion is where Jesus taught his disciples how to pray, and in it he revealed right goals.

Our Father in heaven, hallowed be your name, Your kingdom come, your will be done, on earth as it is in heaven. (Matthew 6:9-10 ESV)

H. Remember that having *the Giver* is better than having *the gifts*. These goals are the test of having a God-oriented lifestyle of fasting:

1. God's name be hallowed.

---

[5] Piper.

2. God's kingdom come.

3. God's will be done on earth.

III. FASTING FOR BREAKTHROUGH

A. Fasting is one of the quickest ways to reveal what's truly in you. What we trust in and what we value most are brought to the surface.

> *More than any other discipline, fasting reveals the things that control us.*[6] *–Richard Foster*

> *Fasting is a way of revealing to ourselves and confessing to our God what is in our hearts. Where do we find our deepest satisfaction—in God or in his gifts?*[7] *–John Piper*

B. In the situation of Jesus fasting in the wilderness for 40 days, his fast was both a testing and a weapon. Fasting reveals the motivations of the heart and also strikes a blow to the enemy at the same time. When we fast, we are joining with Jesus in the declaration that man does not live by bread alone, but by every word that comes from the mouth of God.

C. Of all the ways Jesus could have fought off Satan in the wilderness during his time of testing, the Spirit led him to fast.

> *[7] So to keep me from becoming conceited because of the surpassing greatness of the revelations,[a] a thorn was given me in the flesh, a messenger of Satan to harass me, to keep me from becoming conceited. [8] Three times I pleaded with the Lord about this, that it should leave me. [9] But he said to me, "My grace is sufficient for you, for my power is made perfect in weakness." Therefore I will boast all the more gladly of my weaknesses, so that the power of Christ may rest upon me. [10] For the sake of Christ, then, I am content with weaknesses, insults, hardships, persecutions, and calamities. For when I am weak, then I am strong. (2 Corinthians 12:7-10 ESV)*

> *[29] Who is weak, and I am not weak? Who is made to fall, and I am not indignant? [30] If I must boast, I will boast of the things that show my weakness. (2 Corinthians 11:29-30 ESV)*

D. Who will accept the invitation into this kind of spiritual violence? Everything is available to you by the Spirit, but you must actively lay hold of it.

---

[6] Foster, Richard J. *Celebration of Discipline: The Path to Spiritual Growth*. San Francisco: HarperSanFrancisco, 1988. Print.
[7] Piper.

Fasting is a call to voluntarily embrace weakness in order to experience more of God's power and presence.[8] –Mike Bickle

From the days of John the Baptist until now the kingdom of heaven has suffered [to allow, permit] violence, and the violent take it by force. (Matthew 11:12 ESV)

E.   Not only has God chosen fasting as a means of experiencing the power of God for personal breakthrough and the overthrow of ungodly appetites, it is also a means of aligning with God for breakthrough in the world around us.

[2] In those days I, Daniel, was mourning for three weeks. [3] I ate no delicacies, no meat or wine entered my mouth, nor did I anoint myself at all, for the full three weeks... [12] Then he said to me, "Fear not, Daniel, for from the first day that you set your heart to understand and humbled yourself before your God, your words have been heard, and I have come because of your words. [13] The prince of the kingdom of Persia withstood me twenty-one days, but Michael, one of the chief princes, came to help me, for I was left there with the kings of Persia, [14] and came to make you understand what is to happen to your people in the latter days. For the vision is for days yet to come." (Daniel 10:2-3, 12-14 ESV)

F.   You are called to move angels and demons!

G.   Modern history reveals powerful examples of the church fasting for breakthrough.

1.   President Lincoln officially called for days of prayer and fasting on multiple occasions throughout the American Civil War.

2.   Upon threat of a French invasion, the king of Britain called for a nation-wide day of prayer and fasting.

Fri. February 6, 1756.—The fast day was a glorious day; such as London has scarce seen since the Restoration. Every church in the city was more than full; and a solemn seriousness sat on every face. Surely God heareth the prayer; and there will yet be a lengthening of our tranquillity.[9] –John Wesley

In a footnote, John Wesley wrote, "Humility was turned into national rejoicing for the threatened invasion by the French was averted."

3.   During the Battle of Britain (Jul–Oct 1940), King George VI called for

---

[8] Bickle, Mike, and Dana Candler. *The Rewards of Fasting: Experiencing the Power and Affections of God.* Kansas City: Forerunner, 2005. Print.
[9] Wesley, John. And John Emory. *The Works of the Reverend John Wesley, A.M.* New York: B. Waugh and T. Mason, 1835. Print.

Sunday, September 8 to be a day of nation-wide prayer and fasting as Nazi Germany was attempting to invade. Prime Minister Winston Churchill identified September 15 (the following Sunday) as "the crux of the Battle of Britain." Hitler failed to take the island of Britain.

H.   A concluding testimony of the power of fasting.

To the honor of God alone I will say a little of my own experience in this matter. I was powerfully converted on the morning of the 10th of October. In the evening of the same day, and on the morning of the following day, I received overwhelming baptisms of the Holy Ghost, that went through me, as it seemed to me, body and soul. I immediately found myself endued with such power from on high that a few words dropped here and there to individuals were the means of their immediate conversion. My words seemed to fasten like barbed arrows in the souls of men. They cut like a sword. They broke the heart like a hammer. Multitudes can attest to this. Oftentimes a word dropped, without my remembering it, would fasten conviction, and often result in almost immediate conversion. Sometimes I would find myself, in a great measure, empty of this power. I would go out and visit, and find that I made no saving impression. I would exhort and pray, with the same result. I would then set apart a day for private fasting and prayer, fearing that this power had departed from me, and would inquire anxiously after the reason of this apparent emptiness. After humbling myself, and crying out for help, the power would return upon me with all its freshness. This has been the experience of my life.[10] *–Charles Finney*

---

[10] Finney, Charles. *Power from on High*. Fort Washington: CLC Publications, 2013. Kindle edition. 13 Feb. 2015.

SECTION 3

Understanding Intercession, Authority, and Justice

"A prayer warrior can pray for a thing to be done without necessarily being willing for the answer to come through himself; and he is not even bound to continue in the prayer until it is answered. But an intercessor is responsible to gain his objective, and he can never be free till he has gained it."

Rees Howells

The Supremacy of Christ and a High Perspective on Prayer

If we are to have a better understanding of prayer and how it can be sustained as a lifestyle, then we must have a much higher perspective of its significance than the usual afterthought that it tends to be.

In order to have a right perspective on prayer, you must begin to give more than just a passing glance at the subject of the end of this age. God's end-times plan must become a topic of fascination and enthusiastic study for all Christians. In it is revealed His church fully operational, fully anointed, fully obedient, fully in agreement with Him, and fully participating with Him. It will be a time of unprecedented persecution yet producing unprecedented harvest. It will be our finest hour.

Knowing that is the trajectory you are on ought to excite you and produce a longing in your heart to move even more in that direction right now.

Prayerlessness indicates a lack of true discipleship and study of the word of God. The church's lack of enthusiasm about prayer is symptomatic of an overall spiritual boredom, which is directly related to a failure of beholding Jesus the God-Man.

> *A prayerless minister is the undertaker for all God's truth and for God's church. He may have the most costly casket and the most beautiful flowers, but it is a funeral, notwithstanding the charmful array. A prayerless Christian will never learn God's truth; a prayerless ministry will never be able to teach God's truth. Ages of millennial glory have been lost by a prayerless church. The coming of our Lord has been postponed indefinitely by a prayerless church. Hell has enlarged herself and filled her dire caves in the presence of the dead service of a prayerless church.[1] –E.M. Bounds*

I.   BEHOLDING THE GOD-MAN—THERE IS ONE SEATED FAR ABOVE

   A.   There are many dimensions revealed of Jesus, his position, and his eternal identity. In it all, the beauty of the Lord is unsurpassable. Beholding his beauty and encountering Him changes us and transforms us.

   In the year that King Uzziah died I saw the Lord sitting upon a throne, <u>high and lifted up</u>; and the train of his robe filled the temple. (Isaiah 6:1 ESV)

   And above the firmament over their heads was the likeness of a throne, in appearance like a sapphire stone; on the likeness of the throne was a likeness with the appearance of <u>a man high above</u> it. (Ezekiel 1:26 NKJV)

---

[1] Bounds, E.M. *The Complete Works of E.M. Bounds on Prayer*. Grand Rapids: Baker Books, 2004. Print.

⁶ "As for me, I have set my King on Zion, my holy hill." ⁷ I will tell of the decree: The Lord said to me, "You are my Son; today I have begotten you. ⁸ Ask of me, and I will make the nations your heritage, and the ends of the earth your possession." (Psalm 2:6-8 ESV)

¹⁸ knowing that you were ransomed from the futile ways inherited from your forefathers, not with perishable things such as silver or gold, ¹⁹ but with the precious blood of Christ, like that of a lamb without blemish or spot. ²⁰ He was foreknown before the foundation of the world but was made manifest in the last times for the sake of you (1 Peter 1:18-20 ESV)

B.   We tend to have a very high view of ourselves and a very low view of God. This is a humanistic perspective and value system that, unfortunately, can be found throughout the church.

C.   Do we really know him?

"Behold, God is great, and we do not know Him..." (Job 36:26 NKJV)

II.   THE GOD-MAN AT THE RIGHT HAND OF THE FATHER GOVERNS HUMAN HISTORY

A.   The prophet Daniel saw a shocking vision.

¹³ "I saw in the night visions, and behold, with the clouds of heaven there came one like a son of man, and he came to the Ancient of Days and was presented before him. ¹⁴ And to him was given dominion and glory and a kingdom, that all peoples, nations, and languages should serve him; his dominion is an everlasting dominion, which shall not pass away, and his kingdom one that shall not be destroyed. (Daniel 7:13-14 ESV)

B.   It is startling that a man, who is fully God, will preside over and administrate human history. The fact that he's fully *man* is the astounding part—not that God would lead human history, but that a man would lead human history in perfection.

¹ Then I saw in the right hand of him who was seated on the throne a scroll written within and on the back, sealed with seven seals. ² And I saw a mighty angel proclaiming with a loud voice, "Who is worthy to open the scroll and break its seals?" ³ And no one in heaven or on earth or under the earth was able to open the scroll or to look into it, ⁴ and I began to weep loudly because no one was found worthy to open the scroll or to look into it. ⁵ And one of the elders said to me, "Weep no more; behold, the Lion of the tribe of Judah, the Root of David, has conquered, so that he can open the scroll and its seven seals." ⁶ And between the throne and the four living creatures and among the elders I saw a

Lamb standing, as though it had been slain, with seven horns and with seven eyes, which are the seven spirits of God sent out into all the earth. ⁷ *And <u>he went and took the scroll from the right hand of him who was seated on the throne.</u>* ⁸ *And when he had taken the scroll, the four living creatures and the twenty-four elders fell down before the Lamb, each holding a harp, and golden bowls full of incense, which are the prayers of the saints. (Revelation 5:1-8 ESV)*

C. The scene is complete. The host of heaven fall down, awestruck at the sight of the Man assuming this supreme position. There he stands with the scroll in his hands, and the golden bowls are full.

III. THE INCENSE AND THE PRAYERS COME TOGETHER

A. The four living creatures and the twenty-four elders are all holding harps and golden bowls. This picture describes an end-times fulfillment of the scene so that we know that, when the time comes, the bowls *are* full. What do these golden bowls contain?

...each holding a harp, and golden bowls full of incense, <u>which are the prayers of the saints</u>. (Revelation 5:8 ESV)

B. In this scene, the prayers and the incense have come together. They are one and the same. However, they were not always the same. Originally they were distinct and separate. Now, they are filled with perfumed incense—the very fragrance of the resurrected Christ Himself identified fully with the bride's prayers on the earth.

C. They have been brought together in a supernatural union. They are mingled together by the death of Christ. This fragrance is then presented before Jesus in fullness and partnership with him as he is ready to open the seals of the scroll.

D. It is *overwhelming* to consider this profound passage where the incense and the prayers are one and the same.

E. Revelation 8:1-5 gives us more detail of the scene in Revelation 5:8. There's a merging of the fragrances of Jesus with the prayers of the Church into one reality before God the Father.

¹ When the Lamb opened the seventh seal, there was silence in heaven for about half an hour. ² Then I saw the seven angels who stand before God, and seven trumpets were given to them. ³ And another angel came and stood at the altar with a golden censer, and he was given <u>much incense</u> to offer <u>with the prayers of all the saints on the golden altar before the throne</u>, ⁴ and the smoke of the *incense, <u>with the prayers of the saints</u>, rose before God from the hand of the angel. ⁵ Then the angel took the censer and filled it with <u>fire from the altar</u> and threw it on the earth, and there were peals of thunder, rumblings, flashes of lightning, and an earthquake. (Revelation 8:1-5 ESV)*

F. The incense is the perfumed fragrance of Christ (2 Co 2:15). Jesus' death and that perfumed reality—the fragrance of the God-Man who died—is joined to the prayers of the Church. Initially, they are separate and distinct, but in Revelation 5:8 they are one. Our prayers are not *like* the incense of Christ. They *are* the incense of Christ in this new reality of heaven and earth.

¹⁴ But thanks be to God, who in Christ always leads us in triumphal procession, and through us spreads the fragrance of the knowledge of him everywhere. ¹⁵ For <u>we are the aroma of Christ to God</u> among those who are being saved and among those who are perishing, ¹⁶ to one a fragrance from death to death, to the other a fragrance from life to life. Who is sufficient for these things? (2 Corinthians 2:14-16 ESV)

G. That reality and that new mysterious union looses the government of God in heaven into the earthly natural realm.

H. There's a throne in heaven where God sits, and the Son is seated at his right hand. The golden altar with burning coals of fire is right before the throne. Mysterious and powerful angels along with living creatures and elders surround the scene and are actively involved in what's really happening. Beloved, this is real. This is not just a colorful story or metaphor. The earthly tabernacle was created to mirror the heavenly one.

³⁴ The Lord said to Moses, "Take sweet spices, stacte, and onycha, and galbanum, sweet spices with pure frankincense (of each shall there be an equal part), ³⁵ and make an incense blended as by the perfumer, seasoned with salt, pure and holy. ³⁶ You shall beat some of it very small, and put part of it before the testimony in the tent of meeting where I shall meet with you. It shall be most holy for you. ³⁷ And the incense that you shall make according to its composition, you shall not make for yourselves. It shall be for you holy to the Lord. (Exodus 30:34-37 ESV)

¹² And he shall take a censer full of coals of fire from the altar before the Lord, and two handfuls of sweet incense beaten small, and he shall bring it inside the veil ¹³ and put the incense on the fire before the Lord... (Leviticus 16:12-13 ESV)

⁷ And Aaron shall burn fragrant incense on it. Every morning when he dresses the lamps he shall burn it, ⁸ and when Aaron sets up the lamps at twilight, he shall burn it, a regular incense offering before the Lord throughout your generations. (Exodus 30:7-8 ESV)

¹ In the year that King Uzziah died I saw the Lord sitting upon a throne, high and lifted up; and the train of his robe filled the temple. ² Above him stood the seraphim. Each had six wings: with two he covered his face, and with two he covered his feet, and with two he flew. ³ And one called to another and said: "Holy, holy, holy is the Lord of hosts; the whole earth is full of his glory!" ⁴ And the foundations of the thresholds shook at the voice of him who called, and the house was filled with smoke. ⁵ And I said: "Woe is me! For I am lost; for I am a man of unclean lips, and I dwell in the midst of a people of unclean lips; for my eyes have seen the King, the Lord of hosts!" ⁶ Then one of the seraphim flew to me, having in his hand <u>a burning coal that he had taken with tongs from the altar</u>. (Isaiah 6:1-6 ESV) (see also Revelation 4)

³ And another angel came and stood at the altar with a golden censer, and he was given much incense to offer with the prayers of all the saints on the golden altar before the throne, ⁴ and the smoke of the incense, with the prayers of the saints, rose before God from the hand of the angel. (Revelation 8:3-4 ESV)

¹¹ But when Christ appeared as a high priest of the good things that have come, then through the greater and more perfect tent (not made with hands, that is, not of this creation)... ²⁴ For Christ has entered, not into holy places made with hands, <u>which are copies of the true things</u>, but into heaven itself, now to appear in the presence of God on our behalf. (Hebrews 9:11, 24 ESV)

IV. PRAYER RELEASES GOVERNMENTAL AUTHORITY OVER THE EARTHLY REALM

A. As the seals are opened, justice is released—impacting all of humanity. We see these themes and trends throughout history in smaller or limited instances, but they will reach their fullest expression in the generation of the Lord's return.

B. In God's economy, justice has two dimensions simultaneously. Both mercy and judgment are accomplished at the same time. In Revelation 5:8, the prayers of the saints are in complete agreement with the Lord's heart in this as they have fully matured through encounter with him—beholding his beauty.

² In that day the branch of the Lord [Jesus] shall be <u>beautiful and glorious</u>, and the fruit of the land shall be the pride and honor of the survivors of Israel. ³ And he who is left in Zion and remains in Jerusalem will be called holy, everyone who has been recorded for life in Jerusalem, ⁴ when the Lord shall have washed away the filth of the daughters of Zion and cleansed the bloodstains of Jerusalem from its midst by <u>a spirit of judgment and by a spirit of burning</u>. ⁵ Then the Lord will create over the whole site of Mount Zion and over her assemblies a cloud by day, and smoke and the shining of a flaming fire by night; for over all the glory there will be a canopy. ⁶ There will be a booth for shade by day from the heat, *and for a refuge and a shelter from the storm and rain. (Isaiah 4:2-6 ESV)*

C. Being in agreement with who he is (worship) develops into an agreement with what he said he would do (prayer/intercession).

D. Justice, judgment and vengeance are synonymous words. They can be understood as God making wrong things right.

E. When Jesus spoke to his disciples about prayer, he described a heavenly reality invading the earthly realm. He directly connected this reality being accomplished through day and night prayer.

⁹ Pray then like this: "Our Father in heaven, hallowed be your name. ¹⁰ Your kingdom come, <u>your will be done</u>, <u>on earth</u> as it is in heaven. (Matthew 6:9-10 ESV)

⁷ And will not God give <u>justice</u> to his elect [shall God not avenge- NKJV], who cry to him day and night? Will he delay long over them? ⁸ I tell you, he will give justice to them speedily. Nevertheless, when the Son of Man comes, will he find faith on earth?" (Luke 18:7-8 ESV)

F. It is the intimacy and agreement of the church (the Bride) with Jesus (the Bridegroom) that releases power in the form of answered prayer. God knows that the agreement is vital in order to prevent offense, fear, and falling away. It is the worshipping church in unity with heaven.

And blessed is he who is not offended because of Me [Jesus]. (Matthew 11:6 NKJV)

⁹ "Then they will deliver you up to tribulation and kill you, and you will be hated by all nations for My name's sake. ¹⁰ And then many will be offended, will betray one another, and will hate one another. (Matthew 24:9-10 NKJV)

G. God will purify His church producing a deep love and intimacy. Pondering and meditating on these themes of justice, judgment and vengeance should in *no way* produce anxiety or fear in the heart of the believer. God has a purification for us so that we *will* be able to stand in that day. His primary motivation is love, and He will act in a way that removes all things that hinder it. While everything that can be shaken is being shaken (Hebrews 12:26-29), we will be entering into profound peace, confidence and awe.

V. **THE NEW SONG LOOSES THE GOVERNMENT OF GOD INTO THE NATURAL ARENA**

⁸ ...each holding a harp, and golden bowls full of incense, which are the prayers *of the saints. ⁹ And they sang a <u>new song</u>... (Revelation 5:8-9 ESV)*

A.   The "new song" is mentioned nine times in scripture.

B.   There are a number of levels to it, but the pinnacle of the new song is that it looses the government of God into the natural realm. Psalm 149 says that it actually releases it in partnership with the God-Man. Scripture describes the scene where the God-Man with the scroll is *not* complete. It's the God-Man with the scroll—with a bride participating in unity with His heart—*with the new song of Psalm 149 loosing what is written in the scroll.*

C.   The Church has only a vague understanding of the reality surrounding the role of singing, the new song, and the governing authority that it releases. This is worthy of energetic study and meditation.

VI.   SEE YOURSELF IN THE STORYLINE

A.   Can you read Revelation 5:8 and see yourself? Can you see your personal contribution to the filling of the golden bowls? You have a vital part to play in the maturing of the church and coming into agreement with the heart of Jesus.

B.   There is something far bigger going on than you realize. It's not just about you liking the way worship feels and when you sense the nearness of God.

C.   Why do you think you're interested in the topic of prayer? It's because God himself is orchestrating all things according to his divine plan. He *will* have a praying church in agreement with his heart. Your interest is evidence of that. How thrilling is it to think that when God is working his plan in the earth, His thoughts include you!

D.   You have been invited into the supreme vocation. The prayer room is the governmental center of the universe. History belongs to the intercessor!

> *Prayer does not fit us for the greater works; prayer is the greater work.*[2] – *Oswald Chambers*

---

[2] Chambers, Oswald. "Daily Devotionals By Oswald Chambers." *My Utmost for His Highest.* 17 Oct 2013. Web.

Ministering to the Heart of God

It has been said that the true reward of an intercessor is not answered prayer; it is knowing God. You were made with relationship with Him, and He is looking for people He can trust. Can you truly say that you care about what God cares about? The quick answer is, "Yes," but the honest answer requires more careful introspection.

"That God seeks intercessors but seldom finds them is plain from the pain of His exclamation through Isaiah...and His protest of disappointment through Ezekiel."[1] –Norman Grubb

> *He saw that <u>there was no man</u>, and wondered that there was no one to intercede; then his own arm brought him salvation, and his righteousness upheld him. (Isaiah 59:16 ESV)*

> *And I sought for a man among them who should build up the wall and stand in the breach before me for the land, that I should not destroy it, <u>but I found none</u>. (Ezekiel 22:30 ESV)*

I. **DO WE KNOW THE BROKEN-HEARTED GOD?**

    A.   In times of crisis, people will often ask, "Where was God?" The underlying accusation in the question is that God apparently did not care about what had happened, and then there is offense because He did not intervene.

    B.   The truth is God does care. He cares more than us. More importantly, His concern is not based in weak human sentiment, and His motivation doesn't diminish with time.

> *[4] For the word of the Lord is upright, and all his work is done in faithfulness. [5] <u>He loves righteousness and justice</u>; the earth is full of the steadfast love of the Lord. (Psalm 33:4-5 ESV)*

> *Righteousness and justice are the foundation of your throne; steadfast love and faithfulness go before you. (Psalm 89:14 ESV)*

> *Righteousness and justice are the foundation of Your throne; <u>mercy and truth go before Your face</u>. (Psalm 89:14 NKJV)*

    C.   So where is He? He's right there, not turning away from painful situations like so many of us do.

---

[1] Grubb, Norman. *Rees Howells: Intercessor*. Fort Washington: Christian Literature Crusade, 1952. Print.

¹⁴ Justice is turned back, and righteousness stands far away; for truth has stumbled in the public squares, and uprightness cannot enter. ¹⁵ Truth is lacking, and he who departs from evil makes himself a prey. The Lord saw it, and it <u>displeased</u> [Hebrew: yara] <u>him</u> that there was no justice. ¹⁶ He saw that there was no man [a human being, a champion], and <u>wondered</u> [Hebrew: shamem] that there was <u>no one to intercede</u>; then his own arm brought him salvation, and his righteousness upheld him. (Isaiah 59:14-16 ESV)

1. <u>Yara</u>- to be broken up (with any violent action); be grievous.[2]

2. <u>Shamem</u>- to be astonished (the primary idea is that of silence, being put to silence), to be appalled, to be stunned.[3]

D. In other words, when God sees injustice in the earth, his heart is *shattered*. He then looks to see if there is anyone in the earth that grieves over it as he does. When he finds no one, he sits *stunned and speechless* that he is the only one who cares.

E. Do we know this God?

Behold, God is great, and <u>we know him not</u>... (Job 36:26 ESV)

II. TAKE A WALK IN THE GARDEN

A. The garden has always been the place of encounter. God planted a garden in Eden, and He placed man there.

And the Lord God planted a garden in Eden, in the east, and there he put the man whom he had formed. (Genesis 2:8 ESV)

B. The river that flowed out of the garden in Eden fed all the land's tributaries. Likewise, the place of encounter feeds all other earthly delights. Therefore Eden, the place of encounter, is the standard for all other pleasures.

A river watering the garden flowed from Eden; from there it was separated into four headwaters. (Genesis 2:10 NIV)

C. Man's primary occupation was to cultivate and tend to the place of encounter with the Lord God. The foundational work of man is to nurture the place of encounter with his Maker. This work will not come through the depth of man's knowledge but through encounter with life—with the living God.

---

[2] "Lexicon: Strong's H3415 - Yara." *Blue Letter Bible.* Web. 07 July 2016.
[3] "Lexicon: Strong's H8074 - Shamem." *Blue Letter Bible.* Web. 07 July 2016.

¹⁵ The Lord God took the man and put him in the garden of Eden to work it and keep it. ¹⁶ And the Lord God commanded the man, saying, "You may surely eat of every tree of the garden, ¹⁷ but of the tree of the knowledge of good and evil you shall not eat, for in the day that you eat of it you shall surely die." (Genesis 2:15-17 ESV)

D.   We are called to join Jesus in the proverbial garden of encounter and fellowship.

³² And they went to a place called Gethsemane. And he said to his disciples, "Sit here while I pray." ³³ And he took with him Peter and James and John, and began to be greatly distressed and troubled. ³⁴ And he said to them, "My soul is very sorrowful, even to death. Remain here and watch." ³⁵ And going a little farther, he fell on the ground and prayed that, if it were possible, the hour might pass from him. ³⁶ And he said, "Abba, Father, all things are possible for you. Remove this cup from me. Yet not what I will, but what you will." ³⁷ And he came and found them sleeping, and he said to Peter, "Simon, are you asleep? Could you not watch one hour? ³⁸ Watch and pray that you may not enter into temptation. The spirit indeed is willing, but the flesh is weak." ³⁹ And again he went away and prayed, saying the same words. ⁴⁰ And again he came and found them sleeping, for their eyes were very heavy, and they did not know what to answer him. ⁴¹ And he came the third time and said to them, "Are you still sleeping and taking your rest? It is enough; the hour has come. The Son of Man is betrayed into the hands of sinners. ⁴² Rise, let us be going; see, my betrayer is at hand." (Mark 14:32-42 ESV)

E.   Jesus is still beckoning disciples to keep watch with him in the darkest hours as he pours his heart out in intercession. Can you imagine being awake, alert, and close enough to hear the Son talking with the Father? Can you imagine being there to comfort him at the moment of his deepest anguish?

F.   Peter, James and John were invited to a profound encounter with Jesus in the garden unlike anything they had ever experienced before. The challenge here is to be a follower who "goes a little farther" with Jesus.

G.   This place of encounter is filled with awe and beauty, but it is not limited to only one type of emotion. How could it be? We serve an emotional God. The Lord is looking for those who will go to the garden with him and remain watchful and close enough to experience all that's on his heart.

³⁷ As he was drawing near—already on the way down the Mount of Olives—the whole multitude of his disciples began to rejoice and praise God with a loud voice for all the mighty works that they had seen, ³⁸ saying, "Blessed is the King who comes in the name of the Lord! Peace in heaven and glory in the highest!"... ⁴¹ And when he drew near and saw the city, he wept over it, ⁴² saying, "Would that you, even you, had known on this day the things that make for peace! But now they are hidden from your eyes. ⁴³ For the days will come upon you, when your enemies will set up a barricade around you and surround you and hem you in on every side ⁴⁴ and tear you down to the ground, you and your children within you. And they will not leave one stone upon another in you, because you did not know the time of your visitation." (Luke 19:37-38, 41-44 ESV)

H. The spirit is willing to respond to the invitation of the Lord. However, the flesh often rejects what it finds in that encounter. Some things are just painful, and we wince and pull away from the experience. The weakness of the flesh is revealed in our unwillingness to identify with the seriousness of the moment because it offends our minds and doesn't feel pleasurable to the shallow surface of our senses.

I. One of the great adventures in life is to discover what's important to God—and then what that means for *you*.

> *For us to be this open and vulnerable to both the pain of the world and the anguish of God is unendurable, unless it is matched with the precise sense of divine vocation.⁴ –Walter Wink*

> *"Your tears are the highway to your destiny." –Lou Engle*

J. Venturing into his heart and emotions gives you windows into your own destiny.

> *"What moves you? What is your passion? Stay close to the burning bush in your life. What burns in you and never goes out? When you find something like that, draw close to it, and you'll hear your name called." –Lou Engle*

> *⁵ Those who sow in tears shall reap with shouts of joy! ⁶ He who goes out weeping, bearing the seed for sowing, shall come home with shouts of joy, bringing his sheaves with him. (Psalm 126:5-6 ESV)*

III. INTRODUCING JESUS AS JUSTICE

A. How does the Lord feel about injustice? This question must be asked, but it must also be *felt* in order to truly understand it. Truth is more than just the printed words on the page that make an impression on our mind.

B. For example, how does the Lord feel about the tragic injustice of *abortion*? This is a controversial topic for many, and it is often a painful one from first-

---

⁴ Wink, Walter. *Engaging the Powers: Discernment and Resistance in a World of Domination.* Minneapolis: Fortress Press, 1992. Print.

hand experience. Much of the church avoids it altogether. For that reason, abortion is a perfect example to consider in light of the scriptures that have been featured.

C.   Please allow me to share here a specific encounter with the Lord on this subject of injustice.

1.   In January, 2013 during a 21-day fast and night watch (praying though the night), Matt Lockett received a prophetic word leading up to the 40th anniversary of Roe v. Wade (the 1973 court case that legalized abortion-on-demand in America). In the encounter, the Lord made known the intensity of his emotions and pain of His heart concerning taking the life of the pre-born.

> *"I saw scales in his hand used for weighing and measuring. As I looked, the Lord allowed me to feel and experience his intense pain, anger and emotion regarding the imbalance of the scales. Somehow I understood that Roe v. Wade represented an unjust tampering with the scales, and as a result we can no longer accurately weigh the value of human life."*
> *–Matt Lockett*

> ***Dishonest scales are an abomination** to the Lord, but a just weight is His delight. (Proverbs 11:1 NKJV)*

> ***Unequal weights** are an abomination to the Lord, and **false scales** are not good. (Proverbs 20:23 ESV)*

> *Shall I acquit the man with wicked scales and with a bag of **deceitful weights**? (Micah 6:11 ESV)*

> *Honest scales and balances belong to the Lord; all the weights in the bag are of his making. (Proverbs 16:11 NIV)*

2.   Take a moment to consider the impact to the United States since Roe v. Wade—an estimated 60 million abortions as of 2016. Current statistics reveal there are 1,058,490 abortions per year.[5]

3.   When we evangelize the lost, we often tell them, "God has a plan for your life." We must realize that the baby in the womb is a real human being created in the image of God with a destiny.

4.   Now consider that this massive number of abortions represents just

---

[5] *Abortion Statistics: United States Data & Trends*. National Right to Life Educational Foundation, 2014. Print.

as many shattered dreams in the heart of God with the consent of the American people. This is a reality that few people dare to grasp or pray about.

D.   Unlike man, the Lord has not become callous and indifferent over time due to our persistent sin and disobedience. Thankfully, his mercies are still new every morning.

> *14 "Therefore, behold, I will allure her, and bring her into the wilderness, and speak tenderly to her. 15 And there I will give her her vineyards and <u>make the Valley of Achor</u> [the place of compromise in Joshua 7] <u>a door of hope</u>. And there she shall answer as in the days of her youth, as at the time when she came out of the land of Egypt. (Hosea 2:14-15 ESV)*

E.   Likewise, the Lord has not become any less determined to act.

F.   The definition of justice in it's simplest form is to make wrong things right. We must look at justice, however, from a larger, heavenly perspective. Mere human sentiment and symbolic gestures can never rectify the greatest injustice of all—man's separation from God. Truly, apart from Jesus, there is no justice.

> *1 <u>Behold my servant</u> [Jesus], whom I uphold, my chosen, in whom my soul delights; I have put my Spirit upon him; he will bring forth justice to the nations. 2 He will not cry aloud or lift up his voice, or make it heard in the street; 3 a bruised reed he will not break, and a faintly burning wick he will not quench; he will faithfully bring forth justice. 4 <u>He will not grow faint or be discouraged till he has established justice in the earth</u>; and the coastlands wait for his law. (Isaiah 42:1-4 ESV)*

G.   We are not here to pursue or promote a humanistic expression of justice, which is actually a *false* justice. In other words, a cool drink of water given to someone right before they go to hell still has the same result. This reality offends the natural mind and a church that is increasingly embracing a shortsighted humanistic mindset.

H.   As the hands and feet of Christ on the earth we absolutely must be concerned about the suffering of the broken and needy, but we cannot substitute care for their temporal sufferings in the place of concern for their eternal souls.

I.   Jesus is our only hope to see true justice in the earth and also to maintain a tender heart throughout our stand in the face of prolonged injustice, opposition and negative outcomes.

> *For violence and hatred dry up the heart itself; the long fight for justice*

exhausts the love that nevertheless gave birth to it... Unprotected by prayer, our social activism runs the danger of becoming self-justifying good works, as our inner resources atrophy, the wells of love run dry, and we are slowly changed into the likeness of the Beast.[6] –Walter Wink

J.   A heart steadily held before the Lord will delight in him and remain faithful for the long haul in spite of the extended time it may take to see justice released.

K.   God gave Israel a model for going to war for an extended period of time. It involved not cutting themselves off from that which gives life. We must fight to win, but we cannot afford to fail because we are operating with short-term mindsets.

[19] "When you besiege a city <u>for a long time</u>, making war against it in order to take it, you shall not destroy its trees by wielding an axe against them. You may eat from them, but you shall not cut them down. Are the trees in the field human, that they should be besieged by you? [20] Only the trees that you know are <u>not trees for food</u> you may destroy and cut down, that you may build siegeworks against the city that makes war with you, until it falls. (Deuteronomy 20:19-20 ESV)

L.   The point is that you must have a consistent source of life to sustain you for the long haul. Although we all hope for swift victories, oftentimes the outcomes take far longer than we anticipate.

M.   A contending prayer culture is one that remains in him in order to produce the kind of fruit necessary to bring true deliverance, true justice and true life to the oppressed.

[4] Abide in me, and I in you. As the branch cannot bear fruit by itself, unless it abides in the vine, neither can you, unless you abide in me. [5] I am the vine; you are the branches. Whoever abides in me and I in him, he it is that bears much fruit, for apart from me you can do nothing. (John 15:4-5 ESV)

---

[6] Wink.

What Is Intercession?

While nearly all Christians have a basic understanding of what prayer is, few actually ponder what intercession is. It tends to be one of those words in the New Testament that is difficult to relate to in our modern church experience. Most of the time prayer and intercession just get grouped in together as the same thing.

The lack of understanding the difference between the two actually leads to further misunderstanding and misuse of the the term. "Intercession" cannot simply be replaced with "prayer." When that happens, a high calling a high calling on the church gets lost.

> *Intercession is spiritual defiance of what is, in the name of what God has promised.[1] –Walter Wink*

> *A prayer warrior can pray for a thing to be done without necessarily being willing for the answer to come through himself; and he is not even bound to continue in the prayer until it is answered. But an intercessor is responsible to gain his objective, and he can never be free till he has gained it. He will go to any lengths for the prayer to be answered through himself. But once a position of intercession has been gained, tested and proved, the intercessor can claim all the blessings on that grade, whenever it is God's will for him to do so.[2] –Rees Howells*

I. WE ARE ALL CALLED TO BE INTERCESSORS

A. As followers of Jesus, the Great Intercessor, we are called to make intercession.

> *[1] First of all, then, I urge that supplications [Greek: deesis], prayers [Greek: proseuche], intercessions [Greek: entunchano- plural of enteuxis], and thanksgivings [Greek: eucharistia] be made for all people, [2] for kings and all who are in high positions, that we may lead a peaceful and quiet life, godly and dignified in every way. [3] This is good, and it is pleasing in the sight of God our Savior, [4] who desires all people to be saved and to come to the knowledge of the truth. (1 Timothy 2:1-4 ESV)*

1. Enteuxis (intercession)- a falling in with, meeting with, a coming together.[3]

2. This word carries a meaning that calls the praying person out of their normal experience and into something different; into the unknown.

---

[1] Wink, Walter. *Engaging the Powers: Discernment and Resistance in a World of Domination.* Minneapolis: Fortress Press, 1992. Print.
[2] Grubb, Norman. *Rees Howells: Intercessor.* Fort Washington: Christian Literature Crusade, 1952. Print.
[3] "Lexicon: Strong's G1783 - Enteuxis." *Blue Letter Bible.* Web. 07 July 2016.

3. Intercessions is a technical term for approaching a king.[4]

Intercession visualizes an <u>alternative future</u> to the one apparently fated by the momentum of current contradictory forces. It infuses the air of a time yet to be into the <u>suffocating atmosphere of the present</u>... New alternatives become feasible. The unexpected becomes suddenly possible, because people on earth have invoked heaven, the home of possibilities, and have been heard. What happens next happens because people prayed.[5] –Walter Wink

B. God is looking for intercessors.

And I sought for a man among them who should build up the wall and <u>stand in the breach before me</u> for the land, that I should not destroy it, but I found none. (Ezekiel 22:30 ESV)

[15] The Lord saw it, and it displeased him that there was no justice. [16] He saw that there was no man, and wondered that there was <u>no one to intercede</u>; (Isaiah 59:15-16 ESV)

The intercessor is God-centered. He is not problem-focused; he is not focused on what man can or cannot do. He has a vision of what God can do. When no intercessor can be found among God's people, it is the supreme mark of failure in our responsibility to God and to our fellow man.[6] –Derek Prince

C. There is a severe lack of understanding in the church of exactly what intercession is. Some think it is simply a more intensified form of prayer, while others have wrongly regarded it as some kind of spiritual gifting or calling for a select group of Christians.

D. Simply adding the label "intercession" to a scheduled time of prayer, program, or activity does not automatically make it intercession—no more than hanging a banner that reads "revival this week" on the front of the church guarantees spiritual renewal. We cannot attend a so-called intercession prayer meeting, remain disengaged from the topic of prayer, leave unchanged, and somehow think we have made intercession.

E. It ought to disturb us when we lightly use the word intercession along with anything that requires very little from us.

Intercession is the burden to become responsible for a prayer given by the

---

[4] "Intercessions - Vine's Expository Dictionary of New Testament Words." *Blue Letter Bible*. Web. 07 July 2016.
[5] Wink.
[6] Prince, Derek. *Secrets of a Prayer Warrior*. Grand Rapids: Chosen, 2009. Print.

Holy Spirit.[7] –Richard Maton

This stand of faith against war in order that the gospel might not be hindered was proved to be God's way of placing upon that company a responsibility from which they could never come free until the enemy that God was dealing with should be destroyed.[8] –Norman Grubb

F.   That being said, the simple fact that prayer rooms are scheduling "intercession sets" and regularly praying for specific topics is a definite indication of taking responsibility. We should rejoice over every one of these efforts.

Impossibility presses upon us, breaks over us, is indeed already present. Impossibility is more possible than everything which we hold to be possible. Miracle is just a word we use for the things the Powers (spiritual opposition) have deluded us into thinking that God is unable to do... In our intercessions we fix our wills on the divine possibility latent in the present moment, and then find ourselves caught up in the whirlwind of God's struggle to actualize it.[9] –Walter Wink

Perhaps believers in general have regarded intercession as just some form of rather intensified prayer. It is, so long as there is great emphasis on the word "intensified"; for there are three things to be seen in an intercessor which are not necessarily found in ordinary prayer: identification, agony and authority.[10] –Norman Grubb

II.   IDENTIFICATION IS THE FIRST LAW OF THE INTERCESSOR

A.   Identification- a feeling that you share and understand the problems or experiences of another person.[11]

B.   Jesus is an intercessor. He modeled identification as an essential element for intercession.

And the Word became flesh and dwelt among us, and we have seen his glory, glory as of the only Son from the Father, full of grace and truth. (John 1:14 ESV)

For we do not have a high priest who is unable to sympathize with our weaknesses, but one who in every respect has been tempted as we are, yet without sin. (Hebrews 4:15 ESV)

[7] Maton, Richard. *Samuel Rees Howells: A Life of Intercession*. ByFaith Media, 2012. Print.
[8] Grubb.
[9] Wink.
[10] Grubb.
[11] Identification. *Merriam-Webster Online Dictionary*. Merriam-Webster, n.d. Web. 27 May 2016.

For you know the grace of our Lord Jesus Christ, that <u>though he was rich</u>, yet for your sake <u>he became poor</u>, so that you by his poverty might become rich. (2 Corinthians 8:9 ESV)

Although he was a son, he learned obedience through what he suffered. (Hebrews 5:8 ESV)

[11] Out of the anguish of his soul he shall see and be satisfied; by his knowledge shall the righteous one, my servant, make many to be accounted righteous, and he shall <u>bear their iniquities</u>. [12] Therefore I will divide him a portion with the many, and he shall divide the spoil with the strong, because he poured out his soul to death and was <u>numbered with the transgressors</u>; yet he <u>bore the sin of many</u>, and <u>makes intercession for the transgressors</u>. (Isaiah 53:11-12 ESV)

But we see him who for a little while was made lower than the angels, namely Jesus, crowned with glory and honor because of the suffering of death, so that by the grace of God <u>he might taste death for everyone</u>. (Hebrews 2:9 ESV)

C.   We, of course, do not replace Jesus as the Intercessor, but we are to follow his example and his lead.

> *[The intercessor] pleads effectively because he gives his life for those he pleads for; he is their genuine representative; he has submerged his self-interest in their needs and sufferings. And as far as possible has literally taken their place.[12] –Norman Grubb*

D.   Intercession is inherently sacrificial in its divine nature.

E.   We must *spiritually* "go somewhere" unfamiliar in order to identify with the thing we are praying for. Many times, God even calls us to *physically* go somewhere in our identification. The Holy Spirit once asked a young leader in a dream, "Are you willing to take your intercession into the center of the plague?"

[24] By faith Moses, when he was grown up, refused to be called the son of Pharaoh's daughter, [25] <u>choosing rather to be mistreated with the people</u> of God than to enjoy the fleeting pleasures of sin. (Hebrews 11:24-25 ESV)

[46] And Moses said to Aaron, "Take your censer, and put fire on it from off the altar and lay incense on it and carry it quickly to the congregation and make atonement for them, for wrath has gone out from the Lord; the plague has begun." [47] So Aaron took it as Moses said and <u>ran into the midst</u> of the assembly.

---

[12] Grubb.

And behold, the plague had already begun among the people. And he put on the incense and made atonement for the people. ⁴⁸ And <u>he stood between the dead and the living</u>, and the plague was stopped. (Numbers 16:46-48 ESV)

III. AGONY IS THE SECOND LAW OF THE INTERCESSOR

A.   The Holy Spirit is an intercessor.

²⁶ Likewise the Spirit helps us in our weakness. For we do not know what to pray for as we ought, but the Spirit himself <u>intercedes for us with groanings</u> too deep for words. ²⁷ And he who searches hearts knows what is the mind of the Spirit, because the Spirit <u>intercedes for the saints</u> according to the will of God. (Romans 8:26-27 ESV)

B.   The Holy Spirit is the only present Intercessor on the earth. He is looking for hearts on which to lay burdens and bodies through which He can suffer and work. We are His dwelling place—our bodies are His temple. It is through us that He carries on this conspicuous work. We become intercessors because of the Intercessor within us.

For those who follow the Lord into intercession, the agony with the subject of the intercession may be placed upon the intercessor in stages, making them share the pain and suffering of those they are praying for. The process of identification and agony in intercession are <u>not theoretical</u>, but become as real and as heavy as the crises that are the subject of the prayer.[13] –Richard Maton

C.   Never waste a crisis! Many times the challenges we face are actually opportunities for the Holy Spirit to lead us into more effective intercession by making our requests less "theoretical." You can pray more powerfully into situations that you yourself have faced. Watch for circumstances in your life that are similar to or mirror the conditions faced by the ones you are praying for. Examples might include financial loss, relational strife, persecution, etc.

D.   In order for the Holy Spirit to intercede effectively through a vessel, He must deal with their wrong motives, natural mindsets, and sinful desires. The self must be crucified.

I have been crucified with Christ. It is no longer I who live, but Christ who lives in me. And the life I now live in the flesh I live by faith in the Son of God, who loved me and gave himself for me. (Galatians 2:20 ESV)

[13] Maton.

No one can begin to intercede until he or she has received the Holy Spirit as a Person. If the Holy Spirit is going to live the life of Christ through a person, there must first be... "A full and complete surrender of the will." The Holy Spirit is the Intercessor on earth; we are only His vessels. If we are full of self or the world, we cannot be full of the Holy Spirit.[14] –Richard Maton

To make the prayer 'real,' the Holy Spirit leads the intercessor into a process of identification with the prayer, through encountering similar situations or by identifying with the subject. This process is costly and leads to the crucifixion of the flesh life. As the crucifixion of self proceeds, intercession begins to gain ground. In this context, intercession will always cost.[15] –Richard Maton

E.   The cleansed vessel becomes fit for the Master's use.

This is the intercessor in action, When the Holy Ghost really lives His life in a chosen vessel, there is no limit to the extremes to which He will take him, in His passion to warn and save the lost.[16] –Norman Grubb

1.   Moses offered himself on behalf of his people.

2.   The Apostle Paul offered himself on behalf of his people.

3.   Isaiah had to go naked and barefoot for three years.

4.   Hosea had to marry a harlot.

5.   Jeremiah was not allowed to marry.

6.   Ezekiel was not allowed to shed a tear for the death of his wife.

IV.   AUTHORITY IS THE THIRD LAW OF THE INTERCESSOR

A.   The point of identifying and experiencing the agony of the process is to come through to a place of authority—a gained position.

B.   Our intercession does not serve as a substitute for another's sin. Instead, our intercession brings us into such an identification with the sufferer that we enter into a prevailing position with God.

C.   The intercessor moves God and gains his or her objective.

---

[14] Maton.
[15] Maton.
[16] Grubb.

Prayer is not to bring the petitioner's will into submission to the unchanging will of God, but prayer is to move God to do something which He otherwise would not do.[17] *–Walter Wink*

The price is paid, the obedience is fulfilled, the inner wrestlings and groanings take their full course, and then "the word of the Lord comes." The weak channel is clothed with authority by the Holy Ghost and can speak the word of deliverance.[18] *–Norman Grubb*

D.   Many have experienced "gifts of faith" in different situations. This is truly a gift from God reflecting His goodness, and we rejoice for it. However, there is no authority or power to lay claim on the same result in other situations. Gifts of faith are just that—they are gifts, and they are not necessarily repeated.

E.   When an intercessor gains a new position of authority, he or she enters into the *grace* of faith. Under the direction of the Holy Spirit, he or she then has a claim in that particular area of need.

V.   PRINCIPLES OF INTERCESSION

A.   The intercessor must embrace the cost of discipleship and be fully surrendered.

[5] For as we share abundantly in Christ's sufferings... [9] Indeed, we felt that we had received the sentence of death. But that was to make us rely not on ourselves but on God who raises the dead. (2 Corinthians 1:5, 9 ESV)

A surrendered life is the cornerstone of all intercession.[19] *–Richard Maton*

B.   The intercessor becomes responsible for prayer and must learn to "pray through" until the intercession is complete.

C.   The intercessor cannot pray prayers based in human reasoning because prayer means answer. What are needed are Holy Spirit prayers.

[14] And this is the confidence that we have toward him, that if we ask anything <u>according to his will</u> he hears us. [15] And if we know that he hears us in whatever we ask, we know that <u>we have the requests that we have asked of him</u>. (1 John 5:14-15 ESV)

D.   The intercessor daily abides in the concern—day and night.

[17] Wink.
[18] Grubb.
[19] Maton.

E. The intercessor maintains their place by abiding in Christ, which includes practical acts of obedience; i.e. fasting, giving, changes in lifestyle, etc.

"If you love me, you will keep my commandments." (John 14:15 ESV)

F. The intercessor learns the principle of death before resurrection.

> *Intercession is costly and the intercessor will discover wave upon wave of evil as he or she prevails upon God, to bind the strong man and witness demonic spiritual systems broken. As the individual confronts the powers of darkness, he or she learns that there is death involved in intercession. There may be setbacks, confusion and defeats, but the focus is never just death, but upon the promise of resurrection. The Spirit of God is gaining ground all the time.[20] –Richard Maton*

G. The intercessor knows that this is a hidden ministry and is often misunderstood.

H. The intercessor engages in spiritual warfare.

*For **we do not wrestle against flesh and blood**, but against the rulers, against the authorities, against the cosmic powers over this present darkness, against the spiritual forces of evil in the heavenly places. (Ephesians 6:12 ESV)*

*[3] For though we walk in the flesh, we are **not waging war according to the flesh**. [4] For the weapons of our warfare are **not of the flesh** but have divine power to destroy strongholds. [5] We destroy arguments and every lofty opinion raised against the knowledge of God, and take every thought captive to obey Christ, (2 Corinthians 10:3-5)*

> *History belongs to the intercessors, who believe the future into being. If this is so, then intercession, far from being an escape from action, is a means of focusing for action and of creating action. By means of our intercessions we veritably cast fire upon the earth and trumpet the future into being.[21] –Walter Wink*

---

[20] Maton.
[21] Wink.

Governmental Intercession: Part 1
Earthly Leaders and the Influences Over Them

A great many Christians fail to view government and governmental leaders from a spiritual perspective. Most of the time, discussion is limited to political views that are usually based on personal preferences and opinions. These leaders and the systems they represent will either promote or oppose policies that line up with the word of God.

When Christians take an apathetic posture or a defeatist attitude toward government, they essentially allow evil and wickedness to run unchecked. A proper understanding of the invisible forces that influence governmental leaders will open your eyes to what's at stake, and it will motivate you to engage and pray for God's will to be done.

I. WE MUST PRAY FOR LEADERS IN POSITIONS OF GOVERNMENTAL POWER AND AUTHORITY

    A. In 1975, Bill Bright, founder of Campus Crusade for Christ, and Loren Cunningham, founder of Youth With a Mission (YWAM), developed a strategy to bring change to a nation by reaching its seven spheres, or "mountains," of societal influence. The seven facets of society that must be reached are: Religion, Family, Education, *Government*, Media, Arts and Entertainment, and Business.

    B. Government is one of the seven mountains of society that must be influenced with the Gospel of Jesus Christ, leading toward transformation and reformation.

> *Proverbs 14:34 states that, "righteousness exalts a nation, but sin is a reproach to any people." Many times, as exemplified in the Old Testament, a nation's moral standards are dependent on those exhibited by its leaders (or predominant political party). While each individual is responsible for his or her own sins, the fact remains that people are greatly influenced by those morals (or lack thereof) that popular leaders adopt.[1] –Cindy Jacobs*

    C. As Christians we are exhorted to pray for governmental leaders regardless of personal opinions and preferences, both when circumstances are favorable and when they're antagonistic.

> *[1] First of all, then, I urge that supplications, prayers, intercessions, and thanksgivings be made for all people, [2] <u>for kings and all who are in high positions</u>, that we may lead a peaceful and quiet life, godly and dignified in every way. [3] This is good, and it is pleasing in the sight of God our Savior, [4] who*

---

[1] "The Seven Mountains of Societal Influence." *Generals International*. Web. 22 July 2016.

desires all people to be saved and to come to the knowledge of the truth. (1 Timothy 2:1-4 ESV)

The great majority of Christians never pray seriously for good government at all. Of the few who do pray for good government, hardly any do so with the scriptural conviction that it is really God's will. Whichever of the these explanations may apply in any given situation, the conclusion remains the same: God has made it possible for Christians by their prayers to ensure good government. Christians who fail to exercise this God-given authority are gravely delinquent–both toward God and toward their countries.[2] –Derek Prince

D.   What was the situation when Paul wrote this instruction to Timothy? Nero was Emperor. The city of Rome burned July 18, A.D. 64, and many believed Nero himself was responsible for the arson. Nero, however, placed blame on the Christians in the city. He tortured and killed multitudes.

But all human efforts, all the lavish gifts of the emperor, and the propitiations of the gods, did not banish the sinister belief that the conflagration was the result of an order. Consequently, to get rid of the report, Nero fastened the guilt and inflicted the most exquisite tortures on <u>a class hated for their abominations, called Christians by the populace</u>... Accordingly, an arrest was first made of all who pleaded guilty; then, upon their information, an immense multitude was convicted, not so much of the crime of firing the city, as of hatred against mankind. Mockery of every sort was added to their deaths. Covered with the skins of beasts, they were torn by dogs and perished, or were nailed to crosses, or were doomed to the flames and burnt, to serve as a nightly illumination, when daylight had expired.[3] –Tacitus

E.   God cares about government. Yes, He cares about these individuals and wants them to be saved, but we must also understand that from their positions of authority these individuals affect countless lives and the direction of nations and cultures.

F.   If prayer cannot affect the government, then Paul would not exhort us to pray for these leaders. This exhortation only makes sense if intercession *has the potential* to be effective.

G.   How does God move the hearts of kings?

The king's heart is a stream of water in the hand of the Lord; he <u>turns it</u> wherever he will. (Proverbs 21:1 ESV)

---

[2] Prince, Derek. *Shaping History Through Prayer and Fasting*. New Kensington: Whitaker House, 1973. Print.
[3] Tacitus, Publius Cornelius. *The Annals, Book XV*. A.D. 62-65.

23 These are the numbers of the divisions of the armed troops who came to David in Hebron to turn the kingdom of Saul over to him, according to the word of the Lord... 32 Of Issachar, men who had <u>understanding of the times</u>, to <u>know what Israel ought to do</u>... (1 Chronicles 12:23, 32 ESV)

If they are prophets, and if the word of the Lord is with them, <u>then let them intercede</u> with the Lord of hosts... (Jeremiah 27:18 ESV)

H.   In other words, when you read between the lines of passages about changing of the hearts of leaders, there you will find the intercessors carrying on their hidden work.

II.   THERE ARE TWO REALMS INFLUENCING GOVERNMENTAL LEADERS

A.   Prayer affects governmental rulers in two realms—the heavenly and the earthly. To understand this reality, we need to understand how the apostles and prophets viewed the governmental systems over the nations. Behind human rulers, angelic and demonic rulers influence their decisions for either righteousness or wickedness.

B.   The reality of these two simultaneous realms becomes clearer when we see the Biblical terms describing these rulers. These terms are used interchangeably between both human and angelic beings.

1.   In the book of Daniel, the words *sar* (prince) and *melek* (king) are used for earthly rulers (Daniel 1:1; 1:7-8; 2:2; 9:6, 9:8; 10:1; 11:5) *and* heavenly rulers (Daniel 10:13; 10:20-21).

2.   In the letters of Paul, the words *hyperecho* (authority), *hyperecho exousia* (governing authorities), *exousia* (authorities, powers), *archon* (rulers, princes), and *arche* (rulers, principalities) are used for earthly rulers (Romans 13:1-3; 1 Ti 2:2) *and* heavenly rulers (Romans 8:38; Ephesians 2:2; 3:10; 6:12; Colossians 1:16, 2:15).

C.   Since rulers in the invisible realm are directly influencing rulers in the visible realm, there are aspects of government that cannot be affected simply by petitions, protests, or votes. Some aspects of government can *only* be affected by prayer and intercession.

Mr. Howells recalled, "We pleaded that because of His covenant with Abraham 4,000 years ago, God would take His people back to their Land, and Palestine should again become a Jewish State." The challenge that came before the College was: if the Jewish people did not go back after the 1914-18 war, would they go back after this one? They saw the hand of God in the setting up of a

United Nations Committee to consider the question of Palestine. There was thanksgiving when the news was published that Britain was going to evacuate the country.

On eleven different days during these two months, prayer was concentrated on the coming United Nations vote. It was touch and go. On the day of voting, November 27, 1947, there was much prayer, but the news came that the partitioning of Palestine had not been carried. The College went back to yet more intense prayer, during which they saw in faith "God's angels influencing those men in the United Nations Conference in New York to work on behalf of God's people," and had full assurance of victory.

When, next day, the news came that the United Nations had passed the partitioning of Palestine by 33 votes to 13, and that the State of Israel was a fact, the College acclaimed it with rejoicing as "one of the greatest days for the Holy Ghost in the history of these 2,000 years. During all those centuries there wasn't a single sign that the country was to be given back to the Jews, who were scattered all over the earth, but now, 4,000 years after His covenant with Abraham, He has gathered all the nations together and made them give much of the land of Palestine back to them."[4] –Norman Grubb

D. The Bible is very clear that through our prayers, God moves angels and demons who in turn move kings, dictators, presidents, senators, judges, and governors. Consider the following examples:

Old Testament Example

1. After seventy years of captivity in Babylon, Daniel offered "prayer and pleas for mercy with fasting" (Daniel 9:3) for the Jews to return to Jerusalem and rebuild the city as prophesied by Jeremiah. As a result of his prayers, an angel came and said, "At the beginning of your pleas for mercy a word went out, and I have come to tell it to you, for you are greatly loved" (Daniel 9:23). What is the command that went out as a result of Daniel's intercession? The angel continued, "Know therefore and understand that from the going out of the word to restore and build Jerusalem..." (Daniel 9:25). It was the command from God to release the exiles and send them back to Jerusalem to rebuild it. As a result of this command, we read that "the Lord stirred up the spirit of Cyrus king of Persia, so that he made a proclamation throughout all his kingdom and also put it in writing" (Ezra 1:1). That proclamation was a royal decree to release the Jewish captives to return to Jerusalem to restore the city.

---

[4] Grubb, Norman. *Rees Howells: Intercessor*. Fort Washington: Christian Literature Crusade, 1952. Print.

2.   So when Daniel fasted and prayed, a command went forth from God's throne room, an angel was dispatched in the heavenly realms, and a king's heart was moved in the earthly realm. The law regarding the Jewish captives was instantly changed.

New Testament Example

1.   A time came when "Herod the king laid violent hands on some who belonged to the church" (Acts 12:1). He had James killed (Acts 12:2) and Peter imprisoned (Acts 12:3-4). So the early church gave themselves to "earnest prayer" (Acts 12:5) regarding this matter. As a result of their prayers, one angel was sent to the prison to free Peter (Acts 12:7-10), and another angel was sent to slay King Herod while sitting upon his throne (Acts 12:21-23). With the political pressures from Herod removed, the gospel spread quickly. "But the word of God increased and multiplied" (Acts 12:24).

2.   So when the early church prayed, angels were dispatched in the heavenly realms, a wicked king was removed in the earthly realm, and the political persecution against the church from Herod at that time was restrained.

E.   At the end of the age, we see that the hidden unholy alliances between earthly and demonic kings are completely revealed. We need to discern these relationships and influences now even while they are unseen.

21 In that day the Lord will punish the powers in the heavens above and the kings on the earth below. 22 They will be herded together like prisoners bound in a dungeon; they will be shut up in prison and be punished after many days. (Isaiah 24:21-22 NIV)

F.   Your call to pray and intercede for governmental leaders means you are contending for the prevailing influence over their minds and hearts. This influence of heaven's purposes can turn situations, cause reversal of bad choices, release justice in unjust circumstances, and break the hold of demonic directions designed to keep people in darkness.

Governmental Intercession: Part 2
When Earthly Leaders Rebel Against God's Ideal

God loves good government. He can certainly use both good governmental leaders as well as wicked ones for his purposes, but that is no excuse to remain indifferent towards the topic of government.

The Lord's church—His *ekklesia* in the earth— have a governing role both now and in the age to come. It is imperative that the church gain a right understanding of how earthly governmental systems are to operate and how those systems relate to God's people who serve within them. Much is at stake, and lives hang in the balance.

¹ First of all, then, I urge that supplications, prayers, intercessions, and thanksgivings be made for all people, ² <u>for kings and all who are in high positions</u>, that we may lead a peaceful and quiet life, godly and dignified in every way. ³ This is good, and it is pleasing in the sight of God our Savior, ⁴ who desires all people to be saved and to come to the knowledge of the truth. (1 Timothy 2:1-4 ESV)

I.   GOD'S IDEAL FOR GOVERNMENTAL SYSTEMS

   A.   There must be some form of government for society. Without it there is lawlessness that leads to the increase of evil and allows for great pain and suffering to be inflicted on mankind.

   In those days <u>there was no king</u> in Israel. Everyone did what was <u>right in his own eyes</u>. (Judges 17:6 ESV)

   (Commentary on Judges 17:6) What was the cause of this corruption: There was no king in Israel, no judge or sovereign prince to take cognizance of the setting up of these images (which, doubtless, the country about soon resorted to), and to give orders for the destroying of them, none to convince Micah of his error and to restrain and punish him, to take this disease in time, by which the spreading of the infection might have been happily prevented. Every man did that which was right in his own eyes, and then they soon did that which was evil in the sight of the Lord. When they were without a king to keep good order among them, God's house was forsaken, his priests were neglected, and all went to ruin among them. See what a mercy government is, and what reason there is that not only prayers and intercessions, but giving of thanks, should be made for kings and all in authority, 1 Tim. 2:1, 2.[1] –Matthew Henry

   B.   God has a purpose for government. It is to restrain wrongdoing and punish

---

[1] "Commentary on Judges 17 by Matthew Henry." *Blue Letter Bible*. Web. 28 July 2016.

wickedness, to promote and extend favor for righteousness.

¹ Let every person be subject to the governing authorities. For there is no authority except from God, and those that exist have been instituted by God. ² Therefore whoever resists the authorities resists what God has appointed, and those who resist will incur judgment. ³ For <u>rulers are not a terror to good conduct, but to bad</u>. Would you have no fear of the one who is in authority? Then do what is good, and you will receive his approval, ⁴ for <u>he is God's servant for your good</u>. But if you do wrong, be afraid, for he does not bear the sword in vain. For he is the servant of God, an avenger who carries out God's wrath on the wrongdoer. ⁵ Therefore one must be in subjection, not only to avoid God's wrath but also for the sake of conscience. (Romans 13:1-5 ESV)

¹³ Be subject for the Lord's sake to every human institution, whether it be to the emperor as supreme, ¹⁴ or to governors as sent by him <u>to punish those who do evil and to praise those who do good</u>. ¹⁵ For this is the will of God, that by doing good you should put to silence the ignorance of foolish people. (1 Peter 2:13-15 ESV)

C.   These passages about submitting to the authorities are often misused by Christians. Many take them to mean that whichever candidate wins or whatever policy exists *must be* the will of God. We must therefore submit to it without question.

D.   We may favor one form of government over another. Truly we can see that some forms are better than others with regard to liberties and freedom, but it depends on your human perspective. In fact, God doesn't endorse one form of government over another because they are all man-made. However, they are all held to His divine standard of righteousness and justice.

Righteousness exalts a nation, but sin is a reproach to any people. (Proverbs 14:34 ESV)

Righteousness and justice are the foundation of your throne; steadfast love and faithfulness go before you. (Psalm 89:14 ESV)

¹ Give the king <u>your justice</u> , O God , and <u>your righteousness</u> to the royal son! ² May he [the earthly king] judge your people with righteousness, and your poor with justice! (Psalm 72:1-2 ESV)

The Lord works righteousness and justice for all who are oppressed. (Psalm 103:6 ESV)

To assert that God created the Powers does not imply that God endorses any particular Power at any given time. God did not create capitalism or socialism, but there must be some kind of economic system. The simultaneity of creation, fall, and redemption means that God at one and the same time upholds *a given political or economic system, since some such system is required to support human life;* condemns *that system insofar as it is destructive of full human actualization; and* presses for its transformation *into a more humane order. Conservatives stress the first, revolutionaries the second, reformers the third.* The Christian is expected to hold together all three.[2] *–Walter Wink*

II.   THE CONSPIRACIES OF MEN AGAINST HEAVEN

A.   All governmental systems and leaders ultimately answer to God's divine standard. The leadership of Jesus is a challenge and an offense to these man-made structures that are so often built upon oppression, violence and greed.

B.   Rebellion manifests itself in the form of conspiracy against God's divine standard for government. Plans are discussed. Vain strategies are developed. Though plotted in secret, they don't understand the utter futility of it all.

¹ Why do the nations rage and the peoples plot in vain? ² The kings of the earth set themselves, and the rulers take counsel together, against the Lord and against his Anointed, saying, ³ "Let us burst their bonds apart *and* cast away their cords *from us." (Psalm 2:1-3 ESV)*

"And you, Solomon my son, know the God of your father and serve him with a whole heart and with a willing mind, for the Lord searches all hearts *and* understands every plan and thought. *If you seek him, he will be found by you, but if you forsake him, he will cast you off forever. (1 Chronicles 28:9 ESV)*

C.   To the conspirators, God's ideals are viewed as shackles preventing man-made government from doing whatever it pleases to serve its own goals and desires. The rebellious seek to break these bonds and cords that have restrained them.

III.   HEAVEN'S RESPONSE TO THE REBELLION OF MAN-MADE GOVERNMENT

A.   Unknown to the rebellious in their plotting and scheming, God responds with laughter at the pointlessness of their plan.

He who sits in the heavens laughs; *the Lord holds them in derision [mockery, to imitate any one's voice in stammering]. (Psalm 2:4 ESV)*

---

[2] Wink, Walter. *Engaging the Powers: Discernment and Resistance in a World of Domination*. Minneapolis: Fortress Press, 1992. Print.

B. Why are their conspiracies pointless? Because God has already set in place a holy king on a holy hill who has supremacy over all things. This throne is unshakeable and unequaled.

> *⁵ Then he will speak to them in his wrath, and terrify them in his fury, saying, ⁶ "As for me, <u>I have set my King on Zion, my holy hill</u>." (Psalm 2:5-6 ESV)*

> *"There is a hill above Capitol Hill. There is a court that is higher than the Supreme Court." –Founding motto of Justice House of Prayer DC*

C. The true identity of this supreme king is revealed. It is none other than the Son of God.

> *I will tell of the decree: The Lord said to me, "<u>You are my Son</u>; today I have begotten you. (Psalm 2:7 ESV)*

D. We know the end of the story. Jesus is the only one found worthy to open the seals of the scroll (Revelation 5:5), which can be understood as the title deed to the earth. It is God's good pleasure to give the earth to him as his inheritance.

> *⁸ Ask of me, and I will make <u>the nations your heritage</u>, and <u>the ends of the earth your possession</u>. ⁹ You shall break them with a rod of iron and dash them in pieces like a potter's vessel." (Psalm 2:8-9 ESV)*

> *¹ My heart overflows with a pleasing theme; I address my verses to the king; my tongue is like the pen of a ready scribe. ² You are the most handsome of the sons of men; grace is poured upon your lips; therefore God has blessed you forever. ³ Gird your sword on your thigh, O mighty one, in your splendor and majesty! ⁴ In your majesty ride out victoriously for the cause of truth and meekness and righteousness; let your right hand teach you awesome deeds! ⁵ Your arrows are sharp in the heart of the king's enemies; the peoples fall under you. ⁶ <u>Your throne, O God, is forever and ever</u>. The scepter of your kingdom is a scepter of uprightness; (Psalm 45:1-6 ESV)*

> *But <u>of the Son he says</u>, "Your throne, O God, is forever and ever, the scepter of uprightness is the scepter of your kingdom. (Hebrews 1:8 ESV)*

E. God has a persistent invitation to governmental leadership. You have a part to play—a message to carry—in this tense time of rebellion against God's divine ideal.

> *¹⁰ Now therefore, <u>O kings, be wise; be warned, O rulers of the earth</u>. ¹¹ Serve the Lord with fear, and rejoice with trembling. ¹² <u>Kiss the Son</u>, lest he be angry, and you perish in the way, for his wrath is quickly kindled. Blessed are all who take*

refuge in him. (Psalm 2:10-12 ESV)

F.   We carry this message in prayer, in intercession, and in preaching.

[18] and you will be dragged before <u>governors and kings</u> for my sake, <u>to bear witness before them</u> and the Gentiles. [19] When they deliver you over, do not be anxious how you are to speak or what you are to say, for what you are to say will be given to you in that hour. (Matthew 10:18-19 ESV)

IV.   UNCHECKED REBELLION

A.   We must recognize that the rebellion of earthly government against the divine ideal always leads to wickedness, oppression, and evil. Demonic influence seeks to use these influential systems to crush humanity and resist God's will in the earth.

It was in March, 1936, that Mr. Howells began to see clearly that Hitler was Satan's agent for preventing the gospel going to every creature. As he said later, "In fighting Hitler we have always said that we were not up against man, but the devil. Mussolini is a man, but Hitler is different. He can tell the day this 'spirit' came into him." For several years Mr. Howells stressed the fact that God must destroy him, if the vision of the Gospel to every creature was to be fulfilled.[3] –Norman Grubb

May 22, 9 a.m. "The world is in a panic today, and certainly we would be too, unless we were quite sure the Lord had spoken to us. The destiny of England will be at stake today and tomorrow."

3:30 p.m. "In a battle such as we are in today, you cannot trust in a meeting or in feelings. We must go back to what God has told us. There is an enemy that <u>we must keep in check</u> until God does the big thing."[4] –Rees Howells

B.   We see that blind submission to governmental leadership could, in fact, leave us ineffective in the earth. In the tension of governmental rebellion against God's divine ideal, we have to break our agreement (spoken or unspoken) with the rebellion and come into agreement with God's will.

C.   A stunning question is posed by God to consider in these times.

Shall the throne of iniquity, which devises evil by law, have fellowship with you? (Psalm 94:20 ESV)

---

[3] Grubb, Norman. *Rees Howells: Intercessor.* Fort Washington: Christian Literature Crusade, 1952. Print.
[4] Grubb.

D.   This is a penetrating question that we must all wrestle with. If our hidden agreements were revealed, we would be shocked by just how much compromise we are willing to live with as long as it benefits us in some secret way.

E.   If the governmental rebellion is allowed to fully mature without opposition, then the aim becomes quite clear.

They band together <u>against the life of the righteous</u> and <u>condemn the innocent to death</u>. (Psalm 94:21)

F.   Not every nation provides the ability for its citizens to exercise influence in the form of voting or protest. However, every citizen of heaven is given the privilege of appealing to the Supreme King on the Holy Hill. Earthly kings might accuse these holy ambassadors of revolution or sedition, but they represent a divine governing authority that collides with all of human history.

⁶ For to us a child is born, to us a son is given; and the government shall be upon his shoulder, and his name shall be called Wonderful Counselor, Mighty God, Everlasting Father, Prince of Peace. ⁷ Of the <u>increase of his government</u> and of peace <u>there will be no end</u>, on the throne of David and over his kingdom, to establish it and to uphold it with justice and with righteousness <u>from this time forth and forevermore</u>. The zeal of the Lord of hosts will do this. (Isaiah 9:6-7 ESV)

⁶ "For thus says the Lord of hosts: 'Once more (it is a little while) I will shake heaven and earth, the sea and dry land; ⁷ and I will <u>shake all nations</u>, and they shall come to the Desire of All Nations, and I will fill this temple with glory,' says the Lord of hosts. (Habakkuk 2:6-7 NKJV)

² It shall come to pass in the latter days that the mountain of the house of the Lord shall be established as the <u>highest of the mountains</u>, and shall be lifted up above the hills; and <u>all the nations shall flow to it</u>, ³ and many peoples shall come, and say: "Come, let us go up to the mountain of the Lord, to the house of the God of Jacob, that he may teach us his ways and that we may walk in his paths." For out of Zion shall go the law, and the word of the Lord from Jerusalem. ⁴ He shall judge between the nations, and shall decide disputes for many peoples; and they shall beat their swords into plowshares, and their spears into pruning hooks; nation shall not lift up sword against nation, neither shall they learn war anymore. ⁵ O house of Jacob, come, let us walk in the light of the Lord. (Isaiah 2:2-5)

SECTION 4

Developing Biblical Community and the Corporate Expression of Prayer

"The more genuine and the deeper our community becomes, the more will everything else between us recede, the more clearly and purely will Jesus Christ and his work become the one and only thing that is vital between us. We have one another only through Christ, but through Christ we do have one another, wholly, and for all eternity."

Dietrich Bonhoeffer

Finding Your Tribe

Advancing the kingdom of God alongside other like-minded believers is powerful and rewarding. Some have described the unique experience of finding this kind of group by saying, "I finally found my tribe!" When you find it, you know it because something resonates within you that confirms your spiritual DNA—the purpose you were created for. Finding your tribe can feel like being given *permission* to be who God has already made you to be.

God is bringing together distinct tribes who will contend for spiritual breakthroughs in the earth. He is giving them grace for unity that bridges diversity, commitment that overcomes compromise, and revelation that silences their critics.

When we talk about developing a culture of contending prayer, there are a few qualities to reach for in finding your tribe.

I. **BE PART OF A GROUP WHO CONSECRATES THEMSELVES IN THEIR GENERATION**

    A. Every generation needs fiery messengers and prophets who will reject the status quo of compromise and put holiness on display as a beacon of hope to all those deceived by the spirit of the age.

        If you would do the best with your life, find out what God is doing in your generation and throw yourself wholly into it. –Arthur Wallis

    B. Before massive movements take place when countless people are swept into a move of God, He raises up forerunners to make a way where there is no way. These forerunners are the countercultural dreamers who defy stereotypes and stand in stark contrast to the culture of compromise around them.

        ***And I raised up** some of your sons for **prophets**, and some of your young men for **Nazirites**. Is it not indeed so, O people of Israel?" declares the Lord. (Amos 2:11 ESV)*

        I was just thirty years old... I told the Holy Spirit I knew of no one who had been called to such a thing in this generation [Nazirite consecration].[1] –Rees Howells

    C. God sets people apart for His special purposes. He is looking for those who will accept their God-given assignment and not treat it as an optional thing. Many people treat the assignments of the Lord as suggestions instead of mandates.

---

[1] Grubb, Norman. *Rees Howells: Intercessor*. Fort Washington: Christian Literature Crusade, 1952. Print.

⁶ And the angel of the Lord solemnly assured Joshua, ⁷ "Thus says the Lord of hosts: If you will walk in my ways and <u>keep my charge</u> [watch, assignment], then you shall rule my house and have charge of my courts, and I will give you the right of access among those who are standing here. (Zechariah 3:6-7 ESV)

²² And now, behold, I am going to Jerusalem, constrained by the Spirit, not knowing what will happen to me there, ²³ except that the Holy Spirit testifies to me in every city that imprisonment and afflictions await me. ²⁴ But I do not account my life of any value nor as precious to myself, if only I may finish my course and <u>the ministry that I received</u> from the Lord Jesus, to testify to the gospel of the grace of God. (Ac 20:22-24 ESV)

The world became our parish and we were led <u>to be responsible</u> to intercede for countries and nations.[2] –Rees Howells

Was there anywhere else in the whole of Britain, or America, or elsewhere among God's people another such company, maybe a hundred strong, who were on their knees day by day holding fast the victory by faith while soldiers across the water were retreating mile by mile, whole countries surrendering, and the enemy within sight of their goal? [during World War II][3] –Norman Grubb

II. BE PART OF A GROUP WHO PRIORITIZES PRAYER

A. Jesus' disciples knew what they needed most. They didn't ask to be taught how to be better leaders or how to be more eloquent speakers. They asked him how to pray.

Now Jesus was praying in a certain place, and when he finished, one of his disciples said to him, "Lord, teach us to pray, as John taught his disciples." (Luke 11:1 ESV)

Prayer does not fit us for the greater works; prayer is the greater work.[4] – Oswald Chambers

History belongs to the intercessor.[5] –Walter Wink

Intercession is the supreme vocation. –Lou Engle

---

[2] Grubb.
[3] Grubb.
[4] Chambers, Oswald. "Daily Devotionals By Oswald Chambers." *My Utmost for His Highest*. N.p., 17 Oct 2013. Web. 20 Oct 2013.
[5] Wink, Walter. *Engaging the Powers: Discernment and Resistance in a World of Domination*. Minneapolis: Fortress Press, 1992. Print.

B.   Do you know how to move heaven?

> *The highest form of Christian service is intercessory prayer. The high water mark of spiritual experience is an intercessory life. I care not how emphatically you may boast of your spiritual experience and of the special gifts you have received, your ministry is void of power in the sight of God if you know not how to intercede on behalf of others. The Throne life is what counts.*[6] *–Samuel Howells*

III.   BE PART OF A GROUP WHO PURSUES THE HIGHER PURPOSES OF UNITY AND AGREEMENT WITH EACH OTHER

A.   The Lord has called you to be *corporately* effective and not just *individually* successful. Power in prayer is released through corporate agreement. There are a lot of prayer people out there who "fly solo" because of offense in their heart toward leaders and other brethren. Division and offense ultimately limit your effectiveness in prayer.

> *[18] Truly, I say to you, whatever you bind on earth shall be bound in heaven, and whatever you loose on earth shall be loosed in heaven. [19] Again I say to you, <u>if two of you agree</u> on earth about anything they ask, <u>it will be done for them</u> by my Father in heaven. [20] For where two or three are gathered in my name, there am I among them." (Matthew 18:18-20 ESV)*

B.   The great need for corporate agreement cannot be overemphasized. It is the operational requirement for the effective church, and yet it is often the missing element in most endeavors.

> *The constitution of a community is <u>more important</u> than the passion of its worship or the fervency of its prayers. –Lou Engle*

C.   Unity is essential regardless of the size or scale of your group. Jesus related it to as few as only two people (he knew how difficult it actually is). Imagine the potential if larger groups—whole churches—pressed in for supernatural unity.

D.   Agreement in prayer is something we must contend for and a precious thing that must be fiercely guarded. This is not to create any sense of being exclusive or elite within the body of Christ. Instead, it reflects a desire to be most effective in our God-given assignments.

> *Samuel was also careful concerning whom he prayed with at the College.*

---

[6] Maton, Richard. *Samuel Rees Howells: A Life of Intercession*. ByFaith Media, 2012. Print.

Moses had to pray outside the camp (Exodus 33:7), when the multitudes were not in faith. Inviting untested strangers into "an intercessory prayer meeting," to pray with those who had surrendered all seemed to be inconsistent with the principles of full surrender and the life of abiding. How could they have the faith of God operating through them, if they had never surrendered and invited the Holy Spirit to believe through them? How could visitors only pray the prayers of the Holy Spirit, if they had never met Him personally? How could an unholy or compromised believer become one with a prayer of the Holy Spirit?[7] –Richard Maton

E. In spite of the church's efforts to promote relationships, many people fail to develop close ties and personal bonds that hold them accountable. This kind of isolation must intentionally end because it prevents you from engaging in the mission you are called to.

F. Even though it is largely misunderstood and mocked by fearful critics, God is even raising up expressions of communal living for the purpose of unique effectiveness. Living in community is the quickest way to expose petty differences, wrestle through prejudices, and be quickly humbled in moments of pride and arrogance. While this kind of living arrangement may not be for everyone, in some missions it is entirely appropriate and necessary.

G. Conflict, offense, and unforgiveness are massive hindrances to answered prayer. Contending for godly community is essential for effective prayer.

H. In other words, you need to know who you can go to *lunch* with and who you can go to *war* with.

IV. BE PART OF A GROUP WHO PURSUES THE COUNSEL OF THE LORD

A. There is a big difference between having a good idea and having a "God idea."

[16] Thus says the Lord of hosts: "Do not listen to the words of the prophets who prophesy to you, filling you with vain hopes. They speak visions of their own minds, not from the mouth of the Lord. [17] They say continually to those who despise the word of the Lord, 'It shall be well with you'; and to everyone who stubbornly follows his own heart, they say, 'No disaster shall come upon you.'" [18] For who among them has <u>stood in the council</u> of the Lord <u>to see and to hear his word</u>, or who has paid attention to his word and listened? (Jeremiah 23:16-18 ESV)

B. God releases prophetic insight and information to those who are close to Him.

---

[7] Maton.

"For the Lord God does nothing without <u>revealing his secret</u> to his servants the prophets." (Amos 3:7 ESV)

Of Issachar, men who had <u>understanding of the times</u>, to know what Israel ought to do, 200 chiefs, and all their kinsmen under their command. (1 Chronicles 12:32 ESV)

<u>If they are prophets</u>, and if the word of the Lord is with them, <u>then let them intercede</u> with the Lord of hosts, that the vessels that are left in the house of the Lord, in the house of the king of Judah, and in Jerusalem may not go to Babylon. (Jeremiah 27:18 ESV)

C.   What's need most right now is a church functioning as a prophetic witness—not a corporation with a well-executed business plan.

D.   King David learned the hard way that the "God idea" can be very different than the good idea. The unique presence of God could not be carried by the worldly idea he borrowed from the Philistines—placing the ark of God on an ox cart. Disaster and delay was the result of his leadership when he failed to inquire of the Lord.

⁷ And <u>they carried the ark of God on a new cart</u>, from the house of Abinadab, and Uzzah and Ahio were driving the cart... ¹² And David was afraid of God that day, and he said, "<u>How can I bring the ark of God home to me?</u>" ¹³ So David did not take the ark home into the city of David, but took it aside to the house of Obed-edom the Gittite. ¹⁴ And the ark of God remained with the household of Obed-edom in his house <u>three months</u>. And the Lord blessed the household of Obed-edom and all that he had. (1 Chronicles 13:7, 12-14 ESV)

V.   BE PART OF A GROUP WHO WILL IMPACT NATIONAL AND WORLD EVENTS

A.   Many local churches rarely extend their vision beyond the families of their own congregations. Larger churches or mega-churches might talk about having a city-wide reach. We usually look to the largest organizations with the most plentiful resources, and we leave it to them to have the larger assignments.

B.   We all need to get delivered of this wrong mindset that you have to be big to have a big impact.

C.   You can be small by anyone's standard of measurement, with no resources or finances, but still have "a world vision."

D.   Small is the new big!

Community That's Rooted in Love

Jesus taught that prayer is meant to be answered as two or more agree together. This is a glorious promise. However, to assume that God grants answers to prayer through casual agreement is to underestimate the importance that God places on the law of love operating at the center of our relationships.

If we aim to see the full authority of prayer operating through the corporate body of Christ, then we must lay hold of what Jesus spoke of—what agreement actually looks like.

The apostles of the early church clearly understood this. Together, they pursued inward transformation and renewal into the character of Christ through prayer, studying the Word, prophecy, communion and prophetic ministry (Acts 2:42).

They placed love at the forefront; love that provoked consecration and confronted sin; love that bore one another's burdens and silenced gossip and envy. This apostolic community overflowed in power as they functioned as the "house of prayer for all nations" that Jesus spoke about.

Breakthrough was released in their midst, not simply as a result of their ministry model, but as a result of the Holy Spirit operating through the lifestyles they pursued—"together in one accord" (Acts 1:14; 2:1) centered around Christ. This might sound like a fairytale, but this ministry of the Holy Spirit is still available today. The Holy Spirit is searching for communities who will get a radical vision to live intentionally to apprehend apostolic community.

I.   THE LORD IS BUILDING HIS HOUSE

     A.   The Lord is committed to building His house. What kind of house is the Lord building? We must totally commit to building what God builds (Matthew 7:24-29). He is committed to restoring families and the house of God centered around prayer, devotion and the outworking of love in our relationships.

         Unless the Lord builds the house, those who build it labor in vain... (Psalm 127:1 ESV)

         [19] So then you are <u>no longer strangers and aliens</u>, but you are <u>fellow citizens</u> with the saints and <u>members of the household of God</u>, [20] built on the foundation of the apostles and prophets, Christ Jesus himself being the cornerstone, [21] in whom the whole structure, being <u>joined together</u>, <u>grows into</u> a holy temple in the Lord. [22] <u>In him you also are being built together</u> into a dwelling place for God by the Spirit. (Ephesians 2:19-22 ESV)

         [1] So put away all malice and all deceit and hypocrisy and envy and all slander.

² Like newborn infants, long for the pure spiritual milk, that by it you may grow up into salvation... ⁴ <u>As you come to him</u> [Jesus], a living stone rejected by men but in the sight of God chosen and precious, ⁵ <u>you yourselves like living stones are being built up as a spiritual house</u>, to be a holy priesthood, to offer spiritual sacrifices acceptable to God <u>through Jesus Christ</u>. (1 Peter 2:1-5 ESV)

B.   Jesus Christ is the "cornerstone" that the Body of Christ is "joined together" in like living stones—not dead bricks—that grow into a spiritual house. The purpose of this "spiritual house" is for the sake of functioning as a holy priesthood to offer spiritual sacrifices that God accepts. This is the unique picture of biblical community that the apostles embraced and taught.

⁴² And they devoted themselves to the apostles' teaching and the fellowship, to the breaking of bread and the prayers. ⁴³ And awe came upon every soul, and many wonders and signs were being done through the apostles. ⁴⁴ And all who believed were together and had all things in common. ⁴⁵ And they were selling their possessions and belongings and distributing the proceeds to all, as any had need. ⁴⁶ And day by day, attending the temple together and breaking bread in their homes, they received their food with glad and generous hearts, ⁴⁷ praising God and having favor with all the people. And the Lord added to their number day by day those who were being saved. (Acts 2:42-47 ESV)

C.   Scripture declares that only in the "dwelling together" (to abide, to sit, to be married, to cause cities to be inhabited) of unified prayer is there a commanded blessing to be attained.

Behold, how good and pleasant it is when brothers dwell in unity!... For there the Lord has commanded the blessing, life forevermore. (Psalm 133:1-3)

II.   **INTERCESSION FLOWING FROM THE REVELATION OF JESUS CHRIST**

¹⁵ He said to them, "But who do you say that I am?" ¹⁶ Simon Peter replied, "You are the Christ, the Son of the living God." ¹⁷ And Jesus answered him, "Blessed are you, Simon Bar-Jonah! <u>For flesh and blood has not revealed this to you, but my Father who is in heaven</u>. ¹⁸ And I tell you, you are Peter, and <u>on this rock I will build my church</u> [ekklesia], and the gates of hell shall not prevail against it. ¹⁹ I will give you the keys of the kingdom of heaven, and <u>whatever you bind on earth shall be bound in heaven, and whatever you loose on earth shall be loosed in heaven</u>." (Matthew 16:15-19)

A.   The identity of Jesus is the crucial subject in the generation of the Lord's return. Just as Jesus asked Peter in Matthew 16, *"Who do you say that I am,"* so it will be asked of the final generation (Matthew 24:34). In that moment, Peter shattered a torrent of confusion about Jesus' identity, thundering forth: *"You are the Christ, the Son of the Living God!"* There are pivotal lessons to be learned here that should shape our ecclesiology.

1. "Flesh and blood did not reveal this..."

    Jesus not only commended Peter's response, but also the means by which he received it: "...flesh and blood did not reveal this to you, but My Father who is in heaven." (Matthew 16:13-19). Jesus went on to declare that the entirety of the Church is founded upon this rock—the revelation of Jesus. Revelation should be the aim of believers, not just information. We need understanding regarding the means by which we receive revelation, by the Spirit from God in Heaven (Ephesians 1:17-19).

2. "Upon this rock..."

    Individual or corporate devotion will never ascend beyond the knowledge of the Person to whom we are devoted. If Jesus is to be our chief devotion, where the vision of Jesus is dim and obscure, true adoration will be rare, the wells of love will run dry, and our fervent cries of intercession will be frail and scarce. Yet where Christ is cherished, exalted and revealed in the hearts of the people, then corporate agreement in worship, prayer and devotion will take root with staying power.

3. "I will build my church" (Greek: *ekklesia*)

    In describing the Church, Jesus used the Greek word *ekklesia*. In Greek culture the *ekklesia* was a governmental ruling body of people, charged with authority to make rulings for the larger body. Jesus was declaring that the church was to function as His governing, representative body to "bind" in prayer demonic ideologies—which aim to exalt themselves above the knowledge of God—or to "loose" in prayer agreement, which exalts Christ.

4. "Binding and loosing..."

    Jesus declared that the identity of the redeemed is to function as a *house of prayer for all nations*. This is the decree of the Father in heaven (Isaiah 56:7). The revelation of Jesus—His divinity, His supremacy, His Kingship— is meant to produce agreement through prevailing prayer in the Body of Christ that binds and looses in heaven and on earth.

B. Agreement in prayer is Jesus' requirement to see the fullness of God's purposes manifest at the end of the age. If authority is found only in agreement, we must know what true agreement actually looks like.

III. AGREEMENT IN PRAYER

A. Jesus holds such a high value of prayer and relationships that he places a prerequisite upon answered prayer. He will not grant answers to prevailing prayer at the expense of leaving wounded relationships unaddressed.

18 Truly, I say to you, whatever you bind on earth shall be bound in heaven, and whatever you loose on earth shall be loosed in heaven. 19 Again I say to you, if two of you <u>agree</u> [Greek: symphoneo] on earth about anything they ask, it will be done for them by my Father in heaven. 20 For where two or three are gathered in my name, there am I among them." (Matthew 18:18-20 ESV)

1. *Symphoneo* means to be in accord or to be in harmony. The word "symphony" actually comes from *symphoneo*. In describing agreement in prayer that *binds and looses*, Jesus was speaking of something more than a mere mental assent to a prayer focus; He was describing the constitution of a community.

    The constitution of a community is more important than the passion of its worship or the fervency of its prayers. –Lou Engle

2. The context of Matthew 18 is that of walking in humility, removing offenses, the confession of sins and forgiving one another. Jesus was expounding on the revelation of the *ekklesia* in Matthew 16:15-19. Essentially he was declaring, *"If you want to see wickedness and evil bound on earth and My glory and power released in your midst—on earth as it is in heaven—you must get a heavenly vision for your relationships, and walk in it."*

3. You cannot bind that which binds you.

    We are never called to intercede for sin; that has been done once and for all. But we are often called to intercede for sinners and their needs, and the Holy Ghost can never 'bind the strong man' through us on a higher level than that in which He has first had victory in us.[1] –Rees Howells

B. What kind of prayer does God hear?

1. In Isaiah 58, God exposes unholy heart motivations at work in the middle of prayer and fasting.

    3 'Why have we fasted, and you see it not? Why have we humbled ourselves, and you take no knowledge of it?' Behold, in the day of your fast you seek

---

[1] Grubb, Norman. *Rees Howells: Intercessor*. Fort Washington: Christian Literature Crusade, 1952. Print.

your own pleasure, and oppress all your workers. ⁴ Behold, you fast only to quarrel and to fight and to hit with a wicked fist. Fasting like yours this day will not make your voice to be heard on high. ⁵ Is such the fast that I choose, a day for a person to humble himself? Is it to bow down his head like a reed, and to spread sackcloth and ashes under him? Will you call this a fast, and a day acceptable to the Lord? (Isaiah 58:3-5 ESV)

2. There is nothing more hypocritical than God's people operating in an assuming spirit in prayer and fasting. These hidden motives and neglected areas of love, righteousness and justice must be addressed and repented of.

⁶ "Is not this the fast that I choose: to loose the bonds of wickedness, to undo the straps of the yoke, to let the oppressed go free, and to break every yoke? ⁷ Is it not to share your bread with the hungry and bring the homeless poor into your house; when you see the naked, to cover him, and not to hide yourself from your own flesh? ⁸ <u>Then shall your light break forth like the dawn, and your healing shall spring up speedily; your righteousness shall go before you</u>; the glory of the Lord shall be your rear guard. ⁹ Then you shall call, and the Lord will answer; you shall cry, and he will say, 'Here I am.' (Isaiah 58:6-9 ESV)

3. God promises to release healing and righteousness in our midst when we do. It is conditional: *"If* you will, *then* I will..."

If you take away the yoke from your midst, the pointing of the finger, and speaking wickedness, ¹⁰ if you pour yourself out for the hungry and satisfy the desire of the afflicted, then shall your light rise in the darkness and your gloom be as the noonday. ¹¹ And the Lord will guide you continually and satisfy your desire in scorched places and make your bones strong; and you shall be like a watered garden, like a spring of water, whose waters do not fail. (Isaiah 58:9-11 ESV)

IV. THE PRIMACY OF LOVE IN BIBLICAL COMMUNITY

A. The testimony of Scripture, from the Old Testament prophets to the New Testament Apostles, makes it clear: Jesus puts the primacy of love at the forefront of prevailing intercession. Agreement must be intentionally pursued in our relationships as an expression of the First Commandment.

B. These three remain: faith, hope and love. But the greatest of these is love.

1. Jesus highlighted the primacy of love over every other thing. In connecting the primacy of love to the revelation of the *ekklesia*, he was declaring

something profound. This is the true key to effectual, fervent intercession: Love over service, love over labor, and love over repentance.

2.   A repentance-centric Gospel is a radically diminished Gospel. God is not just asking for people to simply quit doing sinful things. He's requiring that they stop belittling His worth by gorging themselves on inferior pleasures. He is requiring that we respond in the deepest of love for Him. This is a command.

C.   God's heart is attracted to a community of intercession and fasting that gets a vision for "tearing their hearts and not their garments." (Joel 2:12-16).

1.   Torn hearts are a massive contrast to torn garments. This shows the contrast between the external and internal. God is not asking for external displays of holiness and boisterous offerings of prayer. God is looking for inward agreement with His Word and Spirit.

2.   In stark contrast, the disciples and apostles in the early church understood this cry in God's heart throughout the ages. God has called believers to glorify the Godhead with *one mind and one mouth* rooted in the revelation of Jesus Christ, forsaking worldy passions as pilgrims, sojourners, strangers, aliens and sons of the resurrection.

⁴ For <u>whatever was written in former days was written for our instruction</u>, that through <u>endurance</u> and through the <u>encouragement of the Scriptures we might have hope</u>. ⁵ May the God of endurance and encouragement grant you to live in such harmony with one another, in accord with Christ Jesus, ⁶ that <u>together you may with one voice glorify the God and Father of our Lord Jesus Christ</u>. (Romans 15:4-6 ESV)

"But we will devote ourselves to prayer and to the ministry of the word." (Acts 6:4 ESV)

D.   Like the early church in the book of Acts, God desires to build communities of prayer "together in one accord." Being together in one accord means more than everyone doing the same activity in one location. We must get intentional about removing anything that would hinder love for God and love for one another. There is nothing more hypocritical than praying for a baptism of revival when you have bitterness in your heart toward another believer in the prayer meeting.

¹³ until we all attain to <u>the unity of the faith and of the knowledge of the Son of God</u>, to mature manhood, to <u>the measure of the stature of the fullness of Christ</u>, ¹⁴ so that we may no longer be children, tossed to and fro by the waves *and carried about by every wind of doctrine, by human cunning, by craftiness in deceitful schemes. (Ephesians 4:13-14 ESV)*

E.   In Acts 2, the believers in the upper room became fully aware of the indwelling Spirit in them and one another as evidenced by the fire above their heads. Apostolic community is rooted in this understanding: that God dwells not only in my little human frame, but also in my brothers and sisters in Christ. If we saw that same fire of the Spirit resting over each of our heads today, it would be a lot harder to be filled with envy, jealousy, bitterness, and gossip about other believers with whom we are meant to run after God.

Whatever we know of His gifts, His manifestations and His anointings, He is greater than all those. In whatever way He has manifested Himself to us, we also recognize His mighty working in and through others. Increasingly we look to the Holy Ghost Himself, poured out on all flesh, as Joel prophesied, as the only One by whom the Vision He has shown us can be fulfilled, through His prepared channels in all parts of the world... Through this falling of the fire upon the sacrifice, the Spirit had sealed to Himself a company of intercessors for every creature. Tutors and school teachers, doctors and nurses, domestic and office workers, gardeners and mechanics—their duties were varied, but their commission one. Many of the students themselves remained on as part of this praying and working company. There are times in God's dealings with His servants when He sets apart for Himself, not just individuals, but companies, baptized, as it were, by one Spirit into one body for one God-appointed purpose, and this was now one of them.[2] –Dr. Kingsley Priddy, Headmaster, Bible College of Wales

F.   What is the standard of true unity?

Has it ever occurred to you that one hundred pianos all tuned to the same fork are automatically tuned to each other? They are of one accord by being tuned, not to each other, but to another standard to which each one must individually bow. So one hundred worshipers [meeting] together, each one looking... to Christ, are in heart nearer to each other than they could possibly be were they to become 'unity' conscious and turn their eyes away from God to strive for closer fellowship.[3] -A.W. Tozer

G.   Pursue forgiving love in the midst of community.

In the little annoyances of daily life, we are watchful not to excuse the hasty temper, the sharp word, the quick judgment, with the thought that we mean no harm, that we do not keep the anger long, or that it would be too much to

---

[2] Grubb.
[3] Tozer, A.W. *The Pursuit of God*. Chicago: Moody Publishers, 2006. Print.

expect from feeble human nature, that we should really forgive the way God and Christ do. No, we take the command literally, 'Even as Christ forgave, so also do ye.' The blood that cleanses the conscience from dead works, cleanses from selfishness too; the love it reveals is pardoning love, that takes possession of us and flows through us to others. Our forgiving love to men is the evidence of the reality of God's forgiving love in us, and so the condition of the prayer of faith.[4] –Andrew Murray

[4] Murray, Andrew. *With Christ in the School of Prayer*. Springdale: Whitaker House, 1981. Print.

Cultivating Community

The normal church experience for many people bears very little resemblance to the church described in the Bible. Something has been lost in translation, and the distortion has led to a serious lack of effectiveness lasting for generations.

I.   CHURCH IS AN IDEA LOST IN TRANSLATION

A.   Our modern-day understanding of church has become a faint shadow of what is described in the New Testament. In seeking truth, any comparison must be made with what is revealed in scripture and not our contemporary examples. The community of Christian believers described in the book of Acts is a picture of profound and supernatural unity and purpose. Remember that Jesus is building right now toward a glorious reality that culminates in unity on a global scale.

B.   The word church (*ekklesia* in the original Greek) has been culturally handed down to us and has become so common in our modern society that few actually understand its origin or what it really means. Its definition has become distorted from the original intent. The vast majority of people associate it with a building in their neighborhood that serves as a gathering place on Sunday mornings.

> *Ekklesia- There is no clear instance of its being used for a place of meeting or of worship, although in post-apostolic times it early received this meaning. Nor is this word ever used to denote the inhabitants of a country united in the same profession, as when we say the "Church of England," the "Church of Scotland," etc.*[1]

C.   This notion that a church is merely property can be traced historically. The genesis of this idea began with King James in 1604 when he ordered the translation of the Bible into English (completed in 1611). King James heavily influenced the translation of key passages in order to suit his own personal desire for control and to prevent his own position as head of the Church of England from possibly being challenged by an inspired group of peasants.

D.   The English word "church" is translated from the original Greek word *ekklesia*. Our modern use of the word "church" is of little significance in understanding *ekklesia* in the New Testament.

1.   *Ekklesia* is used 118 times in the New Testament. Of those it is translated

---

[1] "Church - Easton's Bible Dictionary." *Blue Letter Bible*. Web. 20 July 2016.

as "church" 114 times and as "assembly" 4 times.

2. The normal usage of the Greek word in New Testament times was understood to simply mean a "called out" or "special assembly." The word *ekklesia* does not automatically denote who is assembling, and thus a modifier is used to describe what particular body was assembled.

    a. In Acts 19:32, 39, 41, the word *ekklesia* is used, but it is modified to denote the kind of assemblies gathered. In this case, civil assemblies and local townspeople. The word "church" clearly would not work here.

    b. In Acts 7:38, it is modified to denote the nation of Israel. The word "church" clearly would not work here.

3. In the New Testament era, society used such words as *thiasos* and *synagoge* to denote fellowships. Our current understanding of the word "church" as it is used in our English Bible is best reverse translated to the late Greek word *kyridakon*, not *ekklesia*. The Greek word *kyridakon* is not found in the New Testament and only came into being in the 16th Century long after New Testament times. Clearly something has become distorted.

E. Our common mindset today allows us to participate in church—where we go to a place on Sunday morning, sit and listen to one person speak, and remain isolated in an unhealthy way with our individualistic boundaries unchallenged. Certainly this is not what Jesus had in mind to execute his divine strategy in challenging the gates of hell.

II. UNDERSTANDING THE BIBLICAL CONCEPT OF *EKKLESIA*

A. Jesus said he was going to build his *ekklesia*. It would be made up of people who are "called out" from among the population and given governing authority. This is an incredibly high calling that gives us a glimpse of our destiny.

[15] He said to them, "But who do you say that I am?" [16] Simon Peter replied, "You are the Christ, the Son of the living God." [17] And Jesus answered him, "Blessed are you, Simon Bar-Jonah! For flesh and blood has not revealed this to you, but my Father who is in heaven. [18] And I tell you, you are Peter, and on this rock I will build my church [Greek: ekklesia], and the gates of hell shall not prevail against it. [19] I will give you the keys of the kingdom of heaven, and whatever you bind on earth shall be bound in heaven, and whatever you loose on earth shall be loosed in heaven." (Matthew 16:15-19 ESV)

** ***¹⁵ "If your brother sins against you, go and tell him his fault, between you and him alone. If he listens to you, you have gained your brother. ¹⁶ But if he does not listen, take one or two others along with you, that every charge may be established by the evidence of two or three witnesses. ¹⁷ If he refuses to listen to them, tell it to the*** <u>***church***</u> ***[Greek: ekklesia]. And if he refuses to listen even to the*** <u>***church***</u> ***[ekklesia], let him be to you as a Gentile and a tax collector. ¹⁸ Truly, I say to you, whatever you bind on earth shall be bound in heaven, and whatever you loose on earth shall be loosed in heaven. ¹⁹ Again I say to you, if two of you agree [Greek: symphoneo] on earth about anything they ask, it will be done for them by my Father in heaven. ²⁰ For where two or three are gathered in my name, there am I among them." (Matthew 18:15-20 ESV)***

1. <u>Ekklesia</u>- a gathering of citizens called out from their homes into some public place, an assembly.[2]

2. <u>Symphoneo</u>- to be harmonious.[3]

B. Explaining how the church would be able to fulfill their mission, Jesus spoke of it in the context of maintaining healthy, close relationships that do not impede their divine function. Relationship is key. Maintaining agreement is vital.

C. As you can see, the function of the church depended on maintaining right relationships in order for many parts to operate in harmony with one another.

D. Disturbances in relationship and agreement hinders the ability of the *ekklesia* to fulfill its mission. A good example would be the covenantal relationship between a husband and wife, which ought to be a picture of agreement—two becoming one flesh.

    Likewise, husbands, live with your wives in an understanding way, showing honor to the woman as the weaker vessel, since they are heirs with you of the grace of life, <u>***so that your prayers may not be hindered***</u>***. (1 Peter 3:7 ESV)***

E. Agreement is the quality that is to be cherished, cultivated and guarded. It does not come naturally or easily. The word *symphoneo* speaks of the symphony that God is after. A symphony requires much practice and sacrifice to produce a harmony of sounds.

F. Symphonies are also large. Individuals must yield to a conductor in order to play their part with others. Consider that they do not automatically play together simply because everyone is dressed the same way.

[2] "Lexicon: Strong's G1577 - Ekklēsia." *Blue Letter Bible*. Web. 20 July 2016.
[3] "Lexicon: Strong's G4856 - Symphōneō." *Blue Letter Bible*. Web. 20 July 2016.

G. Brothers and sisters seeking Jesus' leadership together is magnetic for the manifest presence of Jesus.

For where two or three are gathered in my name, <u>there am I among them</u>." (Matthew 18:20 ESV)

III. CHRISTIAN COMMUNITY SHOULD NOT BE TAKEN FOR GRANTED

A. We ought to marvel at the picture of the New Testament church and hold it up as a standard in our day.

B. The lives of the apostles and their epistles that gave instruction lacked precedent, cultural definition and wide-spread acceptance. The New Testament church was forged behind enemy lines in the context of persecution and very few resources.

> *The Kingdom is to be in the midst of your enemies. And he who will not suffer this does not want to be of the Kingdom of Christ; he wants to be among friends, to sit among roses and lilies, not with the bad people but the devout people. O you blasphemers and betrayers of Christ! If Christ had done what you are doing who would ever have been spared?[4] –Martin Luther*

C. The Christian community is a supernatural work of God's grace. It is a conspicuous work of the Spirit forming one body out of many parts. There is perpetual strife among men, but supernatural unity is possible under the leadership of Jesus who is the head of the body.

D. In Western civilization, we have trivialized the gathering of the saints, reducing it to a form barely recognizable by New Testament standards. We have severely taken for granted our ability to publicly come together for the purpose of worship, prayer, teaching, exhortation and encouragement.

What then, brothers? When you come together, each one has a hymn, a lesson, a revelation, a tongue, or an interpretation. Let all things be done for building up. (1 Corinthians 14:26 ESV)

[15] Look carefully then how you walk, not as unwise but as wise, [16] making the best use of the time, because the days are evil. [17] Therefore do not be foolish, but understand what the will of the Lord is. [18] And do not get drunk with wine, for that is debauchery, but be filled with the Spirit, [19] addressing one another in psalms and hymns and spiritual songs, singing and making melody to the Lord with your heart, [20] giving thanks always and for everything to God the Father in

---

[4] Bonhoeffer, Dietrich. *Life Together*. New York: HarperCollins Publishers, 1954. Print.

the name of our Lord Jesus Christ. (Ephesians 5:15-20 ESV)

¹² Put on then, as God's chosen ones, holy and beloved, compassionate hearts, kindness, humility, meekness, and patience, ¹³ bearing with one another and, if one has a complaint against another, forgiving each other; as the Lord has forgiven you, so you also must forgive. ¹⁴ And above all these put on love, which binds everything together in perfect harmony. ¹⁵ And let the peace of Christ rule in your hearts, to which indeed you were called in one body. And be thankful. ¹⁶ Let the word of Christ dwell in you richly, teaching and admonishing one another in all wisdom, singing psalms and hymns and spiritual songs, with thankfulness in your hearts to God. ¹⁷ And whatever you do, in word or deed, do everything in the name of the Lord Jesus, giving thanks to God the Father through him. (Colossians 3:12-17 ESV)

E. Simply getting together, hanging out, or just being in the same place together does not satisfy the requirements of church. The community of Christians—unto *ekklesia*—requires the supernatural work of the Spirit expressed through willing and active participants seeking unity under the leadership of Jesus. For too long we have lived out church as a matter of routine and never-ending socializing.

F. Jesus is building his *ekklesia*. He is taking many individual parts and combining them in a masterful way into one single body.

⁴ As you come to him, a living stone rejected by men but in the sight of God chosen and precious, ⁵ you yourselves like living stones are being built up as a spiritual house, to be a holy priesthood, to offer spiritual sacrifices acceptable to God through Jesus Christ. (1 Peter 2:4-5 ESV)

G. Jesus is not building a social club. He is not building a country club. He is not building a singles night club—*Ouch!*

H. Jesus wants to bring supernatural community to your home, to your Bible study or prayer group, and to your local congregation. He won't stop there. Can you see him bringing supernatural community to the collective church of your city and region? In the context of the greatest persecution and trial ever seen on earth, Jesus will join us together in a supernatural community on a global scale. This is the quality of leadership we serve!

¹⁶ "I, Jesus, have sent my angel to testify to you about these things for the churches. I am the root and the descendant of David, the bright morning star." ¹⁷ The Spirit and <u>the Bride say, "Come."</u> And let the one who hears say, "Come." And let the one who is thirsty come; let the one who desires take the water of life without price. (Revelation 22:16-17 ESV)

IV. *EKKLESIA* IS A SUPERNATURAL AND POWERFUL WORK OF UNITY

A. Jesus introduced *ekklesia*. Luke was then tasked with describing what he saw developing, which was without precedent.

B. *Homothymadon* was the Greek word chosen by Luke to describe the development of this unique group of people.

C. The word appears 12 times in the New Testament; 11 of those times are in the book of Acts, which was authored by Luke. It describes something far more profound than merely people being in the same place at the same time.

> *All these with one accord [Greek: homothymadon] were devoting themselves to prayer, together with the women and Mary the mother of Jesus, and his brothers. (Acts 1:14 ESV)*

> *When the day of Pentecost arrived, they were all together [homothymadon] in one place. (Acts 2:1 ESV)*

> *And day by day, attending the temple together [homothymadon] and breaking bread in their homes, they received their food with glad and generous hearts, (Acts 2:46 ESV)*

D. *Homothymadon* is literally translated as "same" and "mind."

> *A unique Greek word...helps us understand the uniqueness of the Christian community. Homothumadon is a compound of two words meaning to "rush along" and "in unison." The image is almost musical; a number of notes are sounded which, while different, harmonize in pitch and tone. As the instruments of a great concert under the direction of a concert master, so the Holy Spirit blends together the lives of members of Christ's church.[5]*

E. The musical description of this word hearkens back to the Greek word *symphoneo*, which Jesus used to describe the kind of agreement needed in prevailing prayer (Matthew 18:19).

F. The only other place that the word appears outside the book of Acts is in an apostolic prayer by Paul in the book of Romans.

> *[5] May the God of endurance and encouragement grant you to live in such harmony with one another, in accord with Christ Jesus, [6] that <u>together</u> [homothymadon] you may <u>with one voice</u> [Greek: stoma] glorify the God and Father of our Lord*

---

[5] "Lexicon: Strong's G3661 - Homothymadon." *Blue Letter Bible*. Web. 20 July 2016.

Jesus Christ. ⁷ *Therefore welcome one another as Christ has welcomed you, for the glory of God. (Romans 15:5-7 ESV)*

G. This is not simply like-mindedness as we have understood it to mean. Rather, it is supernatural one-mindedness.

H. One-mindedness creates movement and activity under the leadership of Christ. *Stoma* means "the mouth" and also "the edge of a sword."⁶ In other words, Christ supernaturally unites his people and puts our hands together on one common spiritual sword to advance his kingdom.

I. One-mindedness is possible only when Christ is the head.

¹⁴ so that we may no longer be children, tossed to and fro by the waves and carried about by every wind of doctrine, by human cunning, by craftiness in deceitful schemes. ¹⁵ Rather, speaking the truth in love, we are to grow up in every way <u>into him who is the head, into Christ</u>, ¹⁶ from whom the whole body, joined and held together by every joint with which it is equipped, when each part is working properly, makes the body grow so that it builds itself up in love. (Ep 4:14-16 ESV)

J. One excellent example of this kind of one-mindedness is the company of believers who served alongside Rees Howells at the Bible College of Wales.

> *Through this falling of the fire upon the sacrifice, the Spirit had sealed to Himself a company of intercessors for every creature. Tutors and school teachers, doctors and nurses, domestic and office workers, gardeners and mechanics, their duties were varied, but their commission one. Many of the students themselves remained on as part of this praying and working company. There are times in God's dealings with His servants when He sets apart for Himself, not just individuals, but companies, baptized, as it were, by one Spirit into one body for one God-appointed purpose, and this was now one of them.⁷ –Norman Grubb*

K. This kind of unity is an expanding movement, not a contracting one. That means it grows outwardly from a few to a greater and greater number.

L. How can we hope to have unity among the brethren when we can't even achieve it in our own local fellowship? How can we expect it in our own church, when we can't even find it in our own home. That being said, a good prayer to pray would be, "I want a movement of supernatural unity in my own home!"

---

⁶ "Lexicon: Strong's G4750 - Stoma." *Blue Letter Bible*. Web. 27 July 2016.
⁷ Grubb, Norman. *Rees Howells: Intercessor*. Fort Washington: Christian Literature Crusade, 1952. Print.

SECTION 5

Advancing with a World Vision and a Biblical End-Times Perspective

"I look upon all the world as my parish."

John Wesley

A Special Note Concerning Israel

As we begin to look at prayer and intercession concerning world evangelization, it is vital that the believer establishes a right perspective concerning the end-times and God's ultimate plans for the Jewish people, the nation of Israel, and the city of Jerusalem.

This is a complex topic that cannot be fully unpacked here. Instead, the notes are meant to introduce the subject of Israel to the reader—in hopes of provoking further study.

It is the conviction of the authors that the end-times Biblical storyline is Middle Eastern-focused; it is Israel-centric, and more specifically it is Jerusalem-centric. From God's perspective, the Jews living in Israel are "at the center of the earth" (Ezekiel 38:12 ESV). Consider also this point of view:

> *"Thus says the Lord God: This is Jerusalem. I have set her in the center of the nations, with countries all around her." (Ezekiel 5:5 ESV)*

This is the startling reality for our generation regardless of where we live on the planet. It begs the question: Does any nation have a national destiny apart from that of Israel's?

Many have asked *where is the United States in Biblical prophecy?* It's a question that stems from the vain assumption that the current "most influential and powerful nation on the earth" must be in there somewhere. This perspective tends to force a shift in God's narrative, to focus more on our own success than on His plan that has been declared by the Old and New Testament prophets.

It could possibly be that the U.S. is not a major player in the end-times events of scripture, or it may simply be a firm reminder that it's not all about us. We must not muddy the waters of prophecy with nationalistic or patriotic preferences.

It is the perspective of the authors that God's end-times plan includes a restoration of the Jewish people to the land promised to Abraham (Genesis 15:17-21) and a final fulfillment of unconditional covenantal promises to him. This is not to be misunderstood as a political preference for Jewish policies over Palestinian ones. God's plan absolutely includes the physical and spiritual descendants of Ishmael, but it does not cancel covenantal promises made to the descendants of Isaac.

We reject any theology or end-times perspective that divests historical Israel of her future completion of covenantal promises and figuratively replaces Israel with "the church." This handling of prophecy and promise is commonly known as "replacement theology" or supersessionism, but it has also been called "fulfillment theology."

We strongly urge the reader to pray for revelation concerning the "mystery" of Israel (Romans 11:25).

God's Plans For Israel and the Church: Part 1
The Enduring Faithfulness to the Everlasting Covenant

The issue of Israel is as central to the Gospel as it was central to Paul's ministry (Acts 28:20). Many Christians fail to recognize that the issue of Israel is the issue of the glory of God and His covenant of grace.

If we would endeavor to lay hold of a right eschatology, we must first lay hold of the truth concerning the future of Israel as it relates to God's plan.

Biblical prophecy has much to reveal about the end-times through the study of the mystery of Israel and the everlasting covenant, the mystery of the Church in God's plans, and the mystery of godliness summed up in Christ Jesus. Scripture confirms scripture.

> *It is high time for Christians to interpret unfulfilled prophecy by the light of prophecies already fulfilled. The curses of the Jews were brought to pass literally; so also will be the blessings. The scattering was literal; so also will be the gathering. The pulling down of Zion was literal; so also will be the building up. The rejection of Israel was literal; so also will be the restoration... Christ will come again to this world with power and great glory.... He will take to Himself His great power and reign, and establish an universal kingdom. He will gather the scattered tribes of Israel, and place them once more in their own land... As He literally rode upon a donkey, was literally sold for thirty pieces of silver, had His hands and feet literally pierced, was numbered literally with the transgressors and had lots literally cast upon His raiment, and all that Scripture might be fulfilled so also will He come, literally set up a kingdom and literally reign over the earth, because the very same Scripture has said it shall be so (Acts 1:11; 3:19-21; Psalm 102:16; Zechariah 14:5; Isaiah 24:23; Jeremiah 30:3,18; Daniel 7:13-14).[1] –J.C. Ryle*

Accordingly, the body of Christ must embrace their duty to understand God's plans concerning the mystery of Israel and the Church.

> *It is the duty of every minister of Christ to explain the mystery of Israel. It is a part of our holy religion. It belongs to the counsel of God. It is inseparably connected with the truth as it is in Jesus. There can be no true and full preaching of the Gospel without explaining the mystery of Israel.[2] -Adolph Saphir*

I.   UNDERSTANDING GOD'S PLAN CONCERNING ISRAEL

    A.   Paul carried an apostolic burden for Israel's salvation.

---

[1] Ryle, J. C. *Coming Events And Present Duties: Being Sermons On Prophetical Subjects*. London: William Hunt, 1867. Print.
[2] Saphir, Adolph. *Christ and Israel; Lectures and Addresses on the Jews*. London: Morgan and Scott, 1911. Print.

I am speaking the truth in Christ—I am not lying; my conscience bears me witness in the Holy Spirit— ² that I have great sorrow and unceasing anguish in my heart. ³ For I could wish that I myself were accursed and cut off from Christ for the sake of my brothers, my kinsmen according to the flesh. ⁴ They are Israelites, and to them belong the adoption, the glory, the covenants, the giving of the law, the worship, and the promises. ⁵ To them belong the patriarchs, and from their race, according to the flesh, is the Christ, who is God over all, blessed forever. Amen. (Romans 9:1-5 ESV)

B.   Paul's apostolic burden for Israel did not originate in Paul's mind, but in the heart of God. In Romans 11, Paul described an urgency and necessity for the Church to understand and cooperate with God's plan for Israel's salvation (Romans 11:25).

¹³ Now I am speaking to you Gentiles... ¹⁷ But if some of the branches were broken off [unbelieving Israel], and you [Gentile believers], although a wild olive shoot, were grafted in among the others [Jews]... ¹⁸ do not be arrogant toward the branches... ²⁰ So do not become proud, but fear. (Romans 11:13, 17-18, 20 ESV)

1.   Paul warned believers against being *ignorant* and *arrogant* toward the Jews and the *mystery* of Israel and the Church in the plans of God.

2.   Paul warns that embracing *ignorance* (v. 25) *arrogance* (v. 18) and *pride* (v. 20) that resists cooperating with God's plans for Israel could result in Gentile believers being cut off (v. 22) from God. This is a very sobering warning, fueled by the jealous love that is in God's heart concerning Israel.

C.   God's mystery refers to His plan that He hid through the ages until He revealed it to the apostles (Ephesians 3:5, 9). We must understand the Lord's plans in order to cooperate with them. Paul exhorts believers to embrace the fear of the Lord regarding God's plans for Israel and Gentile believers.

²⁵ For I do not desire, brethren, that you should be ignorant of this mystery... that blindness in part has happened to Israel until the fullness of the Gentiles has come in. ²⁶ And so all Israel will be saved... (Romans 11:25-26 NKJV)

D.   God's original intent was for Israel to have the primary leadership role in bringing God's salvation to all nations (Genesis 12:3; Deuteronomy 28:1; Isaiah 2:1-4; 43:10-12; 44:8-9). Israel will take the gospel to the nations during the Millennial reign of Christ on the earth (Isaiah 66:18-20).

E.   God's redemptive plan from the very beginning has been directly tied to Israel loving and receiving Jesus as their Messiah. God made known these covenantal promises to Abraham (and his descendants), Moses, David and the prophets. This promise was to the descendants of Abraham, Isaac, and Jacob/Israel and connected to a specific piece of land. Israel and, more specifically, Jerusalem are at the epicenter of God's plans.

For Zion's sake I will not keep silent, and for Jerusalem's sake I will not be quiet, until her righteousness goes forth as brightness, and her salvation as a burning torch. (Isaiah 62:1 ESV)

Jerusalem... is the city of the great King. (Matthew 5:35)

II. GOD'S PLAN FOR ISRAEL AND THE CHURCH: AN EVERLASTING COVENANT

A. The issue of Israel is central to the Gospel storyline. God's dealings with Israel demonstrate His faithfulness to His promises and how far He will go for the sake of redemption and salvation. Ultimately, the question is: "Is God faithful to the promise of His everlasting covenant, or has He changed His mind about Israel?"

B. The covenants throughout Scripture point to the plot lines of the Gospel storyline and their ultimate fulfillment in Jesus Christ. As we connect the dots from the Abrahamic Covenant to the New Covenant, we see that God unfolds and confirms His eschatological framework concerning Israel through the prophetic plotlines that are revealed through the covenants.

1. Abrahamic Covenant

    a. On the tail-end of the Tower of Babel scattering, God finds a man of faith, Abram. We're introduced to their relationship through a prophetic promise that God makes to Abram.

    ² And I will make of you a great nation, and I will bless you and make your name great, so that you will be a blessing. ³ I will bless those who bless you, and him who dishonors you I will curse, and in you all the families of the earth shall be blessed." ⁷ Then the Lord appeared to Abram and said, "To your offspring I will give this land." (Genesis 12:2-3, 7 ESV)

    b. God speaks to Abram three times concerning His promise to bless Abram by making a great nation out of his offspring and giving them land to possess as their inheritance (Genesis 12:2-3, 7; Genesis 13:14-17).

c. Abram finally responds to God reiterating His promise by a crying out to God for an heir—a son. Essentially, Abram says, "What good is all this reward? What I really want is a son to receive my ineheritance!"

> *² But Abram said, "O Lord God, what will you give me, for I continue childless, and the heir of my house is Eliezer of Damascus?" ³ And Abram said, "Behold, you have given me no offspring, and a member of my household will be my heir." ⁴ And behold, the word of the Lord came to him: "This man shall not be your heir; your very own son shall be your heir." (Genesis 15:2-4 ESV)*

d. The Abrahamic Covenant was cut in response to this cry in Abram's heart to have a son who would recive his inheritance. It is a reflection of the cry in God's heart for the same desire: that His Son Jesus will receive His inheritance on earth.

> *⁸ But he said, "O Lord God, how am I to know that I shall possess it?" ⁹ He said to him, "Bring me a heifer three years old, a female goat three years old, a ram three years old, a turtledove, and a young pigeon." (Genesis 15:8-9 ESV)*

> *¹⁸ On that day the Lord made a covenant with Abram, saying, "To your offspring I give this land, from the river of Egypt to the great river, the river Euphrates,¹⁹ the land of the Kenites, the Kenizzites, the Kadmonites, (Genesis 15:18-19 ESV)*

e. The Abrahamic covenant was an ongoing, unconditional, one-sided promise made by God to Abraham and his physical descendants through his son Isaac and Isaac's son Jacob/Israel (Genesis 26:3; Genesis 28:13-15).

f. Not only was the covenant made to Abraham and his descendants, but it was also a promise to receive a "promised land" from the Mediterranean Sea to the Euphrates River to the river of Egypt in the Southwest (Genesis 15:18).

2. Mosaic Covenant (Exodus 19:1-9; 34:27-28)

> *⁵ "Now therefore, if you will indeed obey my voice and keep my covenant, you shall be my treasured possession among all peoples, for all the earth is mine; ⁶ and you shall be to me a kingdom of priests and a holy nation. These are the words that you shall speak to the people of Israel." (Exodus 19:5-6 ESV)*

a. After Israel suffers 400 years of affliction under Egypt (confirming the prophecy of Genesis 15:13), God raises up a deliverer, Moses, and further reveals His covenantal promises concerning Israel.

b. The Mosaic Covenant was a two-sided legal agreement between the Lord and all of Israel. God repeatedly highlighted His desire for a people to walk in covenantal love and obedience to Him by declaring, *"If you will, then I will..."* (see Deuteronomy 4:26-27; Deuteronomy 28).

c. The chief aim in God's heart concerning Israel is to demonstrate His relentless jealous love—to have a people as His own possession, for Israel's salvation by grace through faith in Jesus, and for them to love Him completely in return, in the land that He would give them.

    "Hear, O Israel: The Lord our God, the Lord is one. ⁵ You shall love the Lord your God with all your heart and with all your soul and with all your might. (Deuteronomy 6:4-5 ESV)

d. Israel's residency in the land promised by God was dependent upon their covenantal obedience to the laws given in the Mosaic covenant. Thus, Israel's disobedience had catastrophic consequences. However, God never nullified His promises to Abraham when He made the Mosaic Covenant.

    ³⁰ When you are in tribulation, and all these things come upon you in the latter days, you will <u>return</u> to the Lord your God and <u>obey</u> his voice. ³¹ For the Lord your God is a merciful God. <u>He will not</u> leave you or destroy you or <u>forget the covenant with your fathers that he swore to them</u>. (Deuteronomy 4:30-31 ESV)

    "Know therefore that the Lord your God is God, <u>the faithful God who keeps covenant</u> and steadfast love with those who love him and keep his commandments, to a thousand generations..." (Deuteronomy 7:9 ESV)

e. Paul taught that God's promise to Abraham was not nullified by Israel's disobedience or by the law given through the Mosaic Covenant. He is faithful and all that He promised will come to pass.

    ¹⁶ Now <u>the promises were made to Abraham and to his offspring</u>. *[Isaac, Jacob/Israel- see Genesis 17:15-21; 21:9-13]* ***It does not say, "And to offsprings," referring to many,*** *[Abraham's other sons- see Romans*

9:6-13] but referring to one, "And to your offspring," [ultimately] who is Christ. [17] This is what I mean: <u>the law, which came 430 years afterward, does not annul a covenant previously ratified by God, so as to make the promise void.</u> [18] For if the inheritance comes by the law, it no longer comes by promise; but <u>God gave it to Abraham by a promise.</u> (Galatians 3:16-18 ESV)

f. Paul declared that God's "promise" to Abraham concerning "the land" would find it's total fulfillment through Abraham's offspring, ultimately who is Jesus Christ.

3. Davidic Covenant (2 Samuel 7:8-16)

   a. The Davidic covenant was delivered through the prophet Nathan to King David, where God reiterated the promises to the land made through the Abrahamic Covenant. He also promises David something profound: that one of his descendants will sit and reign on the Throne of Israel in Jerusalem.

   [9] And I will make for you a great name... [10] And I will <u>appoint a place for my people Israel</u> and will <u>plant them</u>, so that they may dwell in their own place and be disturbed no more... [12] I will raise up your offspring after you, who shall come from your body, and I will establish his kingdom... [16] <u>Your throne shall be established forever</u>. (2 Samuel 7:9, 10, 12, 16 ESV)

   Of the increase of his government and of peace there will be no end, <u>on the throne of David and over his kingdom</u>, to establish it and to uphold it with justice and with righteousness from this time forth and forevermore. <u>The zeal of the Lord of hosts will do this</u>. (Isaiah 9:7 ESV)

   "For thus says the Lord: David shall never lack a man to sit on the throne of the house of Israel, (Jeremiah 33:17 ESV)

   [31] And behold, you will conceive in your womb and bear a son, and you shall call his name Jesus. [32] He will be great and will be called the Son of the Most High. And <u>the Lord God will give to him the throne of his father David</u>, [33] and <u>he will reign over the house of Jacob forever</u>, and of his kingdom there will be no end." (Luke 1:31-33 ESV)

4. The following table summarizes these three covenants.

COVENANT	MADE TO	WHAT	UNCONDITIONAL OR CONDITIONAL?	UNILATERAL OR BILATERAL?
Abrahamic	Abraham and his descendants	God will give the specific land of Israel to the people of Israel forever, and the Gentile nations will also be blessed	Unconditional	One-way promise
Mosaic	The corporate nation of Israel	God defined conditions for Israel to maintain residency of the land	Conditional	Two-way agreement
Davidic	King David	God will raise up a descendant of David to sit on the throne of Israel and rule from Jerusalem forever	Unconditional	One-way promise

C.   The New Covenant

1.   Through the New Covenant, we see that God's *ultimate intent* in His covenantal promises was about much more than simply possessing land. The LORD will place His Spirit, His words, His heart into Israel for the sake of salvation.

2.   The New Covenant was *inaugurated* when Jesus—Son of God, Son of David, Holy One of Israel—voluntarily gave His broken body and shed His blood unto death on the Cross, that both Jew and Gentile would be saved by grace through faith in Christ (Romans 10:11-13; 1 Timothy 2:5).

3.   The New Covenant does *not* abrogate God's original plans to corporate Israel. Through Christ, Israel will be saved—by love, for the sake of love—to serve and love Jesus fully, specifically in the land that God promised to give them.

21 Thus says the Lord God: Behold, I will take the people of Israel from the nations among which they have gone, and will... bring them to their own land. 22 And I will make them one nation in the land, on the mountains of Israel. And one king shall be king over them all... 23 I will save them from all the backslidings in which they have sinned, and will cleanse them; and they shall be my people, and I will be their God. (Ezekiel 37:21-23 ESV)

> *Therefore he [Christ] is the mediator of a new covenant, <u>so that those who are called may receive the promised eternal inheritance</u>, since a death has occurred that redeems them from the transgressions committed under the first covenant. (Hebrews 9:15 ESV)*

III. MESSIANIC HOPE

A.   The central plumbline throughout the covenants points to the ultimate promise of the coming Messiah, Jesus. God was faithful to the literal fulfillments of every prophecy concerning the Messiah at the First Advent and so He will do in the Second Advent.

B.   In earth's darkest hours, Messianic hope will pierce through the darkness. The Cross was the greatest expression of the depths of the Father's love and commitment to Israel's salvation. Jesus willingly endured the pain and scorn of the Cross, giving witness to God's ongoing fidelity to the everlasting covenant.

> *The glorious reign of Jesus in the latter day will not be consummated, until a terrible struggle has convulsed the nations. His coming will be as a refiner's fire, and like fuller's soap, and the day thereof shall burn as an oven. Earth loves not her rightful monarch, but clings to the usurper's sway: the terrible conflicts of the last days will illustrate both the world's love of sin and Jehovah's power to give the kingdom to his only Begotten. To a graceless neck the yoke of Christ is intolerable, but to the saved sinner it is easy and light. We may judge ourselves by this: do we love that yoke, or do we wish to cast it from us?[3] –Charles Spurgeon*

C.   From the very beginning, Jesus chose Jerusalem as the place from which He would establish His Throne and reign on the earth.

> *[17] You will bring them in and <u>plant them on your own mountain</u>, the place, O Lord, which you have made for your abode, the sanctuary, O Lord, which your hands have established. [18] The Lord will reign forever and ever." (Exodus 15:17-18 ESV)*

D.   Jesus will return with righteousness and justice, ruling and reigning on the throne of David in Jerusalem. He alone will be the stability of our times. He alone is the Desire of all Nations.

> *"Behold, the days are coming, declares the Lord, when I will raise up for David <u>a righteous Branch</u>, and <u>he shall reign as king</u> and deal wisely, and shall execute justice and righteousness in the land. (Jeremiah 23:5 ESV)*

---

[3] Spurgeon, C. H. *C.H. Spurgeon's Treasury of David - (Psalm 2)*. Grand Rapids: Zondervan, 1940. Print.

...and he will be the stability of your times, abundance of salvation, wisdom, and knowledge; the fear of the Lord is Zion's treasure. (Isaiah 33:6 ESV)

God's Plans For Israel and the Church: Part 2
The Salvation of Israel

The Apostle Paul's teachings on Israel reveal a profound depth of understanding into scripture and an apostolic burden that should shape the Church's posture towards the Jewish people in their past election, present rebellion, and future salvation.

How did Paul look upon the issue of Israel and feel about it? How did it impact his worldview and shape his ministry vision?

In this hour of history, the Church must peer into the issue of Israel. This issue, this "mystery," must be seen throughout scripture; it must be acknowledged; it must be felt; it must be prioritized and not ignored; it must be prayed for. This session is to introduce the general realities contained in Romans 9-11, in hopes that it will fuel the theological and missiological reformation in the Church around the issue of Israel.

I.   HOW DID PAUL LOOK UPON THE ISSUE OF ISRAEL?

    A.   In Romans 9-11, Paul presents seven realities concerning the issue of Israel.

        1.   Agony- Paul felt agony over Israel's spiritual condition (Romans 9:1-5)

> *I am speaking the truth in Christ—I am not lying; my conscience bears me witness in the Holy Spirit— ² that I <u>have great sorrow and unceasing anguish</u> in my heart. ³ For I could wish that I myself were accursed and cut off from Christ for the sake of my brothers, my kinsmen according to the flesh. (Romans 9:1-3 ESV)*

        2.   Purpose- Paul understood God's divine purposes revealed through Scripture for Israel's election and salvation (Romans 9:6-13; 11:1-7)

> *⁶ <u>But it is not as though the word of God has failed.</u> For not all who are descended from Israel belong to Israel, ⁷ and <u>not all are children of Abraham because they are his offspring,</u> but "Through Isaac shall your offspring be named." ⁸ This means that it is not the children of the flesh who are the children of God, but the children of the promise are counted as offspring. ¹¹...in order that God's purpose of election might continue, not because of works but because of him who calls... (Romans 9:6-8, 11 ESV)*

> *<u>I ask, then, has God rejected his people? By no means!</u> For I myself am an Israelite, a descendant of Abraham, a member of the tribe of Benjamin.*

² God has not rejected his people whom he foreknew... ⁵ So too at the present time there is a remnant, chosen by grace. ⁶ But if it is by grace, it is no longer on the basis of works; otherwise grace would no longer be grace. (Romans 11:2, 5-6 ESV)

3.   Prayer- Paul prayed for the manifestaion of God's purpose for Israel in light of their current condition of rebellion and God's promise to Israel of future salvation. (Romans 10:1-3)

Brothers, my heart's desire and prayer to God for them is that they may be saved. (Romans 10:1 ESV)

4.   Preaching- Paul stressed the necessity of preaching to the Jews concerning Christ, for the sake of their salvation (Romans 10:12-21).

¹⁴ How then will they call on him in whom they have not believed? And how are they to believe in him of whom they have never heard? And how are they to hear without someone preaching? ¹⁵ And how are they to preach unless they are sent? As it is written, "How beautiful are the feet of those who preach the good news!" ¹⁶ But they have not all obeyed the gospel. For Isaiah says, "Lord, who has believed what he has heard from us?" ¹⁷ So faith comes from hearing, and hearing through the word of Christ. (Romans 10:14-17 ESV)

5.   Provocation- Paul understood God's plan concerning the Gentile Church provoking Israel to jealousy after Jesus (Romans 11:11-15).

¹¹ So I ask, did they stumble in order that they might fall? By no means! Rather through their trespass salvation has come to the Gentiles, so as to make Israel jealous. ¹² Now if their trespass means riches for the world, and if their failure means riches for the Gentiles, how much more will their full inclusion mean!

¹³ Now I am speaking to you Gentiles. Inasmuch then as I am an apostle to the Gentiles, I magnify my ministry ¹⁴ in order somehow to make my fellow Jews jealous, and thus save some of them. (Romans 11:11-14 ESV)

6.   Prophecy- Paul understood biblical prophecy concerning the future salvation of Israel (Romans 11:25-27).

I do not want you to be unaware of this mystery, brothers: a partial hardening has come upon Israel, until the fullness of the Gentiles has come in. ²⁶ And in this way all Israel will be saved, as it is written, "The Deliverer will come from Zion, he will banish ungodliness from Jacob"; ²⁷

"and this will be my covenant with them when I take away their sins."
(Romans 11:25-27 ESV)

7. Praise- The revelation of God's plans concerning Israel and the Church causes Paul to praise the wisdom and knowledge of God (Romans 11:28-36).

²⁸ As regards the gospel, they are enemies for your sake. But as regards election, they are beloved for the sake of their forefathers. ²⁹ <u>For the gifts and the calling of God are irrevocable</u>. ³³ Oh, the depth of the riches and wisdom and knowledge of God! How unsearchable are his judgments and how inscrutable his ways! (Romans 11:28-29, 33 ESV)

II. THE SALVATION OF ISRAEL—UNDERSTANDING THE 4 PARTS OF GOD'S PLAN

A. The Cross displays the fullness of God's covenantal promises and Jesus' "zeal" and "exceeding jealousy" for Israel, the Gentiles, and Jerusalem as His city— "the city of the Great King." Jesus is zealous for Jerusalem because of what *will* happen there, not only what has happened in the past.

¹³ For the Lord has chosen Zion; <u>he has desired it for his dwelling place</u>: ¹⁴ "This is my resting place forever; here I will dwell, for I have desired it. (Psalm 132:13-14 ESV)

For Zion's sake I will not keep silent, and <u>for Jerusalem's sake I will not be quiet</u>, <u>until</u> her righteousness goes forth as brightness, and her salvation as a burning torch. (Isaiah 62:1 ESV)

¹⁴ So the angel who talked with me said to me, 'Cry out, Thus says the Lord of hosts: <u>I am exceedingly jealous for Jerusalem and for Zion</u>... ¹⁷ the Lord will again comfort Zion and again choose Jerusalem.' (Zechariah 1:14, 17 ESV)

B. In Romans 11, Paul highlighted four parts of God's plan to bring the gospel to the nations. God's plan includes the fullness of the Gentiles (v. 25) and the fullness of Israel (v. 12).

²⁵ For I do not desire, brethren, that you should be <u>ignorant</u> of this mystery... that blindness in part has happened to Israel until the <u>fullness of the Gentiles</u> has come in. ²⁶ And so <u>all Israel will be saved</u>... (Romans 11:25-26 NKJV)

For I am not ashamed of the gospel, for it is the power of God <u>for salvation</u> to everyone who believes, <u>to the Jew first</u> and also <u>to the Greek</u>. (Romans 1:16 ESV)

III. PART ONE- TEMPORARY SPIRITUAL BLINDNESS

A. The Jewish people have a temporary spiritual blindness on them (v. 25).

1. Israel has stumbled (v. 11) through sin and unbelief causing a temporary, partial spiritual blindness even to this day (v. 25). Their blindness includes not being able to see Jesus as their Messiah, as well as being blind to their hostility against Him.

2. However, Paul declares that it is *partial*—a remnant of Jews have been, are being, and will be saved (v. 5)—and it is *temporary*—it will be lifted when the fullness of the Gentiles comes in (v.25).

3. Israel's blindness to and rejection of Jesus is not total (Rom. 11:1-10) and it is not final (Rom. 11:11-32). This blindness (partial hardening) is *until* (v.25). God has an appointed time for salvation, when He will restore Israel's national calling to her primary leadership role of bringing the Gospel to the nations during the millennial reign of Christ (Is. 66:18-20).

4. Ignorance and arrogance (concerning God's purposes for Israel and the temporary, partial spiritual blindness) causes many believers to conclude that God is "finished" or "done" with Israel, which can lead to passive resistance (silence in the face of opposition and persecution of the Jews) and then active resistance (partaking in the persecution of Israel and the Jews), instead of laboring and praying for Israel's salvation and destiny.

IV. PART TWO: FULLNESS OF GENTILES PROVOKING ISRAEL TO JEALOUSY

A. The fullness and salvation of the Gentiles (v. 25) will provoke Israel to seek Jesus for salvation (v. 11). All Israel will be saved (v. 26).

...through their trespass salvation has come to the Gentiles, so as to make Israel jealous. (Romans 11:11 ESV)

1. Salvation- the salvation of the Gentiles speaks not only of individuals being saved, but the Gentiles being used as God's instrument to bring the Gospel to the nations and to the Jews over the last 2,000 years.

2. Fullness- the fullness of the Gentiles speaks of the *full number* of Gentiles who will come to salvation and are walking in *the fullness of the Spirit's power and godly character*—a walk worthy of the Lord (Colossians 1:10; Ephesians 4:1)—that causes them to fulfill *the fullness of God's purposes for them.*

3. Provoking to Jealousy- Gentile believers will walk in the Spirit to such a degree that they will *provoke Israel to godly jealously*—they will jealously

yearn to possess the things of God in the way that they see the Gentiles do. This reality will take place in the context of the suffering of Great Tribulation.

B.   Jesus prophesied about the timeframe of Israel's spiritual blindness, salvation, and embracing of His leadership as Messiah and King, when he will reign from Jerusalem.

1.   Jesus prophesied that He would not return to Jerusalem until the governmental leaders of Israel voluntarily ask Him to reign over them as their Messianic King.

37 "O Jerusalem, Jerusalem... How often would I have gathered your children together... [but] you were not willing! 38 See, your house is left to you desolate. 39 For I tell you, <u>you will not see me again, until you say, 'Blessed is he who comes in the name of the Lord.'</u>" (Matthew 23:37-39 ESV)

2.   Just as the Father "bound" Himself to Israel's leaders by covenanting the land to them (Genesis 15:18) so Jesus "bound" Himself by His prophecy to only come back after Israel's leadership invites Him.

3.   Satan's rage is focused on Israel and the Jews because he believes that he has found a "loophole" in Jesus' prophecy and God's end-time plan. Satan aims to keep the leaders of Israel from receiving Jesus as King, thus proving that Jesus' prophetic word is false. He reasons that if Jesus' prophecy is shown to be a lie, then Jesus can't imprison Satan as a liar.

4.   Thus, Satan has a threefold strategy to undermine God's prophetic plans concerning Israel:

a.   Satan seeks to try and kill the entire Jewish race.

b.   Satan seeks to make the Jewish people so offended at Jesus that they will never receive Him as their king.

c.   Satan seeks the destruction or military occupation of Israel by God's enemies.

19 Repent therefore, and turn back, that your [Israel] sins may be blotted out, 20 that times of refreshing may come from the presence of the Lord, and that he may send the Christ appointed for you, Jesus, 21 whom heaven must receive <u>until the time for restoring all the things</u> about which God spoke by the mouth of his holy prophets long ago. (Acts 3:19-21 ESV)

V. PART THREE: THE SALVATION OF ISRAEL

A. All of the words that Jesus spoke concerning Israel will come to pass. All Israel will be saved (v. 26), and confess that Jesus is their Savior and Messiah.

1. Literally, all of corporate Israel will come to salvation in the context of Jesus' return and his millennial reign. This means that 100% of the Jewish people who survive the Tribulation will believe in Jesus as they are provoked to jealousy and behold His beauty (Zechariah 13:8).

And in this was all Israel will be saved, as it is written: "The Deliverer [Jesus] will come from Zion, and He will banish ungodliness from Jacob [Israel]." (Romans 11:26 ESV)

[16] On that day the Lord their God will save them, as the flock of his people for like the jewels of a crown they shall shine on his land. [17] For how great is his goodness, and how great his beauty! (Zechariah 9:16-17 ESV)

[9] And the Lord will be king over all the earth. On that day the Lord will be one and his name one. (Zechariah 14:9 ESV)

2. Paul's teaching that all Israel will be saved is confirmed by Isaiah (Isaiah 45:17, 25; 59:20; 60:21).

3. Israel will be the first nation that is totally saved and living righteously (Isaiah 60:21).

VI. PART FOUR: FULLNESS OF ISRAEL

A. The fullness of Israel (v. 12) will lead to God's glory filling the millennial earth (v. 15).

For if their rejection is the reconciliation of the world, what will their acceptance be but life from the dead? (Romans 11:15 ESV)

1. Fullness- the fullness of Israel speaks of the full number who will come to salvation and walk in *the fullness of the Spirit's power* and *godly character—a walk worthy of the Lord* (Colossians 1:10; Ephesians 4:1)—causing them to fulfill *the fullness of God's purposes for them.*

2. Life from the dead- If Israel's temporary and partial rejection (v. 15) meant the reconciliation of the world as salvation came to the Gentiles, then Israel's salvation will be extraordinary—Paul likens it to nothing less than *life from the dead* for the whole earth.

VII. HOW SHOULD THE CHURCH RESPOND?

A. How should the Church respond to the plans of God concerning Israel revealed through His Word?

1. Apostolic witness- God's *irrevocable* (v.29) plans are directly tied to Israel loving His Son Jesus. Thus, the plans of the Gentile Church are directly tied to Israel, as well as *the fullness of the Gentiles* (v.12) coming into the Kingdom. To neglect this dimension of biblical prophecy is to embrace a passive response in hastening the Second Coming of Christ (2 Peter 3:12). Therefore, the Church should respond by diligently searching the Scriptures with a desire to humbly, but boldly stand as faithful witnesses to God's eschatological plans for Israel. *What manner of people ought we to be?*

    11...what sort of people ought you to be in lives of holiness and godliness, 12 waiting for and hastening the coming of the day of God, because of which the heavens will be set on fire and dissolved, and the heavenly bodies will melt as they burn! (2 Peter 3:11-12 ESV)

2. Agreement- The international Gentile church must not remain in ignorance and arrogance concerning God's purposes for Israel which can lead to passive resistance (silence in the face of opposition and persecution of the Jews) and then active resistance (partaking in the persecution of Israel and the Jews). Instead, we must humbly agree with God and His purposes. We must repent of any areas where the Church has been arrogant or ignorant of God's plans concerning Israel and the Jewish people.

    28 As regards the gospel, they are enemies for your sake. But as regards election, they are beloved for the sake of their forefathers. 29 For the gifts and the calling of God are irrevocable. 30 For just as you [Gentiles] were at one time disobedient to God but now have received mercy because of their [Jews] disobedience, 31 so they too have now been disobedient in order that by the mercy shown to you they also may now receive mercy. (Romans 11:28-31 ESV)

3. Intercession- The Father promises to establish a global prayer movement to intercede for the salvation of Israel and the future glory of Jerusalem, to usher in this reality on earth. The Church must respond with fervent intercession for the protection and salvation of Israel and for the Father to establish Jerusalem as a praise in the earth.

    6 On your walls, O Jerusalem, I have set watchmen; all the day and all the night they shall never be silent. You who put the Lord in remembrance, take no rest, [7] and give him no rest until he establishes Jerusalem and makes it a praise in the earth. (Isaiah 62:6-7 ESV)

[6] Pray for the peace of Jerusalem! "May they be secure who love you! [7] Peace be within your walls and security within your towers!" [8] For my brothers and companions' sake I will say, "Peace be within you!" [9] For the sake of the house of the LORD our God, I will seek your good. (Psalm 122:6-9 ESV)

Brothers, my heart's desire and prayer to God for them is that they may be saved. (Romans 10:1 ESV)

God is Not Done with America

The United States of America has an undeniably rich Christian heritage with a long history of large-scale revivals that have been invaluable for preserving the nation and directing its corporate conscience. However, current negative trends have led some to think that America is now too far gone—that she has fallen too far to recover what has been lost.

The challenges are real: low church attendance, ineffective youth engagement, pervasive cultural wickedness, the decline of the traditional family, continued legalized abortion on demand, etc. The list goes on and on.

Focusing on everything that is wrong will certainly lead you to a negative conclusion. Scripture declares, though, that God's arm is never too short to save. The stage is set once again for historic revival in America. We can't ignore the *facts*, but we must lay hold of *God's promises*. People of prayer live in the tension between the two. In between what "is" and what "could be," we pray, "Thy kingdom come, thy will be done in earth, as it is in heaven."

I.   PRAYER PRECEDES REVIVAL

A.   Historic revival and great awakening are coming to the United States again. This is both a prophetic declaration and a prayerful plea. Many are now saying that it has already begun. If it has, it is only in its earliest stages of potential.

B.   A crescendo of prayer always precedes revival.

[11] For I know the plans I have for you, declares the Lord, plans for welfare and not for evil, to give you a future and a hope. [12] Then you will call upon me and come and pray to me, and I will hear you. [13] You will seek me and find me, when you seek me with all your heart. (Jeremiah 29:11-13 ESV)

So is God's will, through his wonderful grace, that the prayers of his saints should be one great and principal means of carrying on the designs of Christ's kingdom in the world. When God has something very great to accomplish of this church, it is his will that there should precede it the extraordinary prayers of his people;...And it is revealed that, when God is about to accomplish great things for his church, he will begin by remarkably pouring out the spirit of grace and supplication.[1] –Jonathan Edwards

Oh! men and brethren, what would this heart feel if I could but believe that there were some among you who would go home and pray for a revival: men

---

[1] Edwards, Jonathan. *The Works of Jonathan Edwards, A.M: Volume 1*. London, 1839. Print.

whose faith is large enough, and their love fiery enough to lead them from this moment to exercise unceasing intercessions that God would appear among us and do wondrous things here, as in the times of former generations.[2] – Charles Spurgeon

When God intends great mercy for his people, the first thing he does is to set them a-praying.[3] –Matthew Henry

I continue to dream and pray about a revival of holiness in our day that moves forth in mission and creates authentic community in which each person can be unleashed through the empowerment of the Spirit to fulfill God's creational intentions.[4] –John Wesley

When the revival in Adams, New York, that commenced with his own conversion began to decline, Charles Finney read an article entitled "A Revival Revived." Summarizing it, he wrote, "The substance of it was, that in a certain place there had been a revival during the winter; that in the spring it declined; and that upon earnest prayer being offered for the continued out-pouring of the Spirit, the revival was powerfully revived." He suggested to the young people in his church that they should each pray in their rooms at sunrise, at noon and at sunset for one week. Before the week was out, a marvelous spirit of prayer was poured out on them, some lying prostrate on the floor during these seasons, praying for the outpouring of the Spirit. "The Spirit was poured out, and before the week ended all the meetings were thronged."[5] –Arthur Wallis

C.   We do not look at the current state of the nation and become downcast by its pitiful state or by what seems like powerlessness on the part of the church to affect change.

D.   Instead, we go to prayer over the matter. The real question is, "How badly do you want revival?" Truly desperate times call for desperate measures. It is certainly *not* a time for "business as usual." Our fervent prayers coupled with fasting and intercession pave the way for the breakthrough that is needed.

E.   Can you imagine entire churches given to long seasons of prayer and fasting for breaththrough? What if numerous churches within a city bonded together to pray and fast for the region? It's not a time to think up a new program to try, but it *is* a time to do the things God prescribes that are often neglected.

---

[2] Spurgeon, Charles. *Sermons of Rev. C.H. Spurgeon: Sixth Series*. New York: Robert Carter & Brothers, 1883. Print.
[3] "Zechariah 12 Commentary - Matthew Henry Commentary on the Whole Bible (Complete)." *Bible Study Tools*. Web. 14 July 2016.
[4] Wesley, John. *How to Pray: The Best of John Wesley on Prayer*. Uhrichsville: Barbour, 2007. Print.
[5] Wallis, Arthur. *In The Day of Thy Power*. CLC Publications. Kindle Edition.

Thus says the Lord: "Stand by the roads, and look, and ask for the ancient paths, where the good way is; and walk in it, and find rest for your souls. (Jeremiah 6:16 ESV)

F.   Are God's people being moved to pray and cry out? Is the word of God being preached? Is God still sending messengers? If the answer is yes, then there is still hope.

If what accredited English writers say of that period is even half true, England in the early decades of the eighteenth century was a sorry spectacle, in spite of the fact that it had men of brilliant genius... Just at the hour when the situation was most utterly dark, deplorable, and unpromising, something happened -- a fire broke out, and soon the Methodist poet of awakened, renewed England was singing with ecstatic exultation... Men were saying in that century... as they are saying now, that the day of preaching had gone by, when, lo! a thousand insistent voices were heard along the highways of that 'fair island, set in silver,' and a new day had dawned.[6] –Ezra Squier Tipple

G.   The Lord is raising up intercessors, apostolic preachers, evangelists, and missionaries who will partner with him to see the nation turn back to him. All of our prayers, obedience, overflowing life, and faith-filled risks spill out into the streets. They pour fresh water on the destiny and long-forgotten prophetic promises of America. Salvation will spring up from this ground again!

[7] "For there is hope for a tree, if it be cut down, that it will sprout again, and that <u>its shoots will not cease.</u> [8] Though its root grow old in the earth, and its stump die in the soil, [9] yet <u>at the scent of water</u> it will bud and put out branches like a young plant. (Job 14:7-9 ESV)

II.   **THE PRAYER ROOM IS THE LAUNCH PAD FOR GOD'S PURPOSES**

A.   The house of prayer and the praying church are the "staging ground" for what God wants to do next with this nation.

B.   God divinely leads us in how we can most effectively partner with him to see his divine will fulfilled in the earth.

Therefore pray earnestly to the Lord of the harvest to send out [Greek: ekballo] laborers into his harvest. (Matthew 9:38 ESV)

1.   <u>Ekballo</u>- to cast out, drive out, to send out. To command or cause one to depart in haste.

---

[6] Tipple, Ezra Squier. *Francis Asbury: The Prophet of the Long Road*. The Methodist Book Concern, 1916. Print.

2.   To lead one forth or away somewhere with *a force which he cannot resist.*[7]

C.   It's in the place of prayer that God will impart to you His heart for the nation. He will speak to you there about what He wants to do. In prayer, we can come into agreement with Him and His plans. *That* prayer thrusts forth the agents of His plan into the harvest field.

III.   BREAK OFF REVIVAL CYNICISM

A.   Refuse to be a person of criticism and accusation concerning the possibilities of God visiting America again with great awakening.

> *God is the constant possibility of transformation pressing on every occasion.*[8]
> *–Walter Wink*

> *I have great hope for America because the depth of a fall never determines God's ability to restore. I'm not afraid of the powerful strongholds because size and strength are completely irrelevant when measuring His abilility to deliver. And I'm not intimidated because statistical odds, whether of success or failure, cease to be relevant when God is involved. His limitless ability negates the very concept of "odds," and trumps all other winning hands.*[9]
> *–Dutch Sheets.*

B.   Reject *revival cynicism.* Awakening has come to this nation before, and it will come again!

C.   A study of historical revivals in America is strongly recommended including their conditions, locations and key people involved. A few examples that could serve as an introduction to the topic include:

1.   The First Great Awakening (18th century)

2.   The Second Great Awakening (19th century)

3.   The Cane Ridge Revival (1801)

4.   The Businessman's Revival (1857)

5.   The Azusa Street Revival (1906)

---

[7] "Lexicon: Strong's G1544 - Ekballō." *Blue Letter Bible*. Web. 14 July 2016.
[8] Wink, Walter. *Engaging the Powers: Discernment and Resistance in a World of Domination*. Minneapolis: Fortress Press, 1992. Print.
[9] Sheets, Dutch. *An Appeal to Heaven*. Dallas: Dutch Sheets Ministries, 2015. Print.

6. The Jesus Movement (1960s–1970s)

D. Knowledge of America's revival history helps produce faith for its continuation in the future. It also brings greater understanding for prayers like, "God, send another great awakening," and, "Lord, give us another Jesus Movement."

> *Yes, our nation has a flawed past and perhaps an even more flawed present. But I'm not asking for a merit-based revival where God gives us tokens of His goodness in response to our excellent behavior. Obviously, God isn't going to award America with a revival simply because He's impressed with our actions. But isn't that the point of revival? If we were "good enough," we wouldn't need one![10] –Dutch Sheets*

E. It is important to note that these historic revivals had a profound and direct impact on the release of justice (ending slavery) and the formation of global missionary efforts. We should expect no less from a future awakening in America.

---

[10] Sheets.

Progress of the Heart

The Bible teaches that we are to be people who take great care of the heart. It is the heart that represents both our willingness or our hardness toward God's plans. It is the human heart that processes and holds all the wonderful expressions of God's love like tenderness, compassion, empathy, courage, grief, passion, and zeal.

Blessed are the pure in heart, for they shall see God. (Matthew 5:8 ESV)

It is in the place of prayer that the heart is poured out and gives expression to what is often unexplainable. Therefore, great care must be taken to cultivate a prayer life that enables your heart to be fully alive in God with a capacity for the mission ahead.

I.   **DON'T STOP PRAYING**

A.   When we think about the ultimate assignment—fulfilling the Great Commission—we must keep prayer as a core element of the process.

37 Then he said to his disciples, "The harvest is plentiful, but the laborers are few; 38 therefore <u>pray earnestly to the Lord of the harvest</u> to send out laborers into his harvest." (Matthew 9:37-38 ESV)

The number of missionaries on the field depends entirely on the extent to which someone obeys that command and prays out the laborers.[1] –Andrew Murray

B.   The immensity of the task will pull you in a variety of directions and create a whole host of priorities that, if allowed to, will easily take the place of prayer and intercession. Prayer is essential to fulfilling this mission.

The gospel moves with slow and timid pace when the saints are not at their prayers early and late and long.[2] –E.M. Bounds

C.   The Apostle Paul exhorted us to "pray without ceasing" (1 Thessalonians 5:17). Ceaseless prayer isn't about making non-stop requests. It's about having an ongoing conversation with Jesus Christ, the Great Intercessor.

D.   Your ability to effectively be part of God's plan to evangelize the globe depends on you continually remaining in relationship and communication with Him. It is in the place of daily encounter that you find what is needed to accomplish

---

[1] Grubb, Norman. *Rees Howells: Intercessor.* Fort Washington: Christian Literature Crusade, 1952. Print.
[2] Bounds, E.M. *The Complete Works of E.M. Bounds on Prayer: Experience the Wonders of God through Prayer.* Grand Rapids: Baker Books, 2004. Print.

the mission before you.

The Lord, the God of their ancestors, sent word to them through his messengers __again and again__ [Greek: shakam; rising up betimes- KJV], because he had pity on his people and on his dwelling place. But they mocked God's messengers, despised his words and scoffed at his prophets until the wrath of the Lord was aroused against his people and there was no remedy. He brought up against them the king of the Babylonians, who killed their young men with the sword in the sanctuary, and did not spare young men or young women, the elderly or the infirm. God gave them all into the hands of Nebuchadnezzar. (2 Chronicles 36:15-17 NIV)

E. This passage gives us a fascinating picture of God. It actually says that He gets up early every day—translated here as "again and again"—and forms a plan.

1. <u>Shakam</u>- to rise or start early.

2. Before the usual or expected time. An inconvenient time.

3. Properly, to incline (the shoulder to a burden); literally, to load up (on the back of man or beast), i.e. to start early in the morning:—(arise, be up, get (oneself) up, rise up) early (betimes), morning.[3]

F. In other words, God gets up early in the morning every day and puts together His great mercy strategy. Faithful messengers and witnesses have also risen at the inconvenient time to see and to hear this plan.

For who among them has stood in the council of the Lord to see and to hear his word, or who has paid attention to his word and listened? (Jeremiah 23:18 ESV)

G. These messengers who are prepared in this secret place of encounter carry more than just words. These holy heralds actually carry God's heart. In this place of encounter, God places the burdens of his heart onto those who will faithfully carry them from that place. What a privilege it is to get to be a part of this divine plan and to personally know His mercies are new every morning!

The steadfast love of the Lord never ceases; his mercies never come to an end; they are __new every morning__; great is your faithfulness. (Lamentations 3:22-23 ESV)

II. WHAT IS THE CAPACITY OF YOUR HEART?

---

[3] "Lexicon: Strong's H7925 - Shakam." *Blue Letter Bible.* Web. 13 July 2016.

A. You must cultivate a heart that's prepared for the mission by encountering God's heart. There's a big difference between "watching and praying" versus "waiting and playing."

B. The sad truth today is that you can make it speedily to the mission field and yet arrive with a heart that is unprepared for the mission. You need more than just the *willingness* to go. You will need a heart that has the capacity for the mission God has called you to.

C. A pioneering spirit will fling you to the world, but in the modern age, we lack a mode of travel that fosters a vibrant prayer life. The efficiencies of travel and the abundance of resources have fundamentally changed the process of missions in a dramatic way. It is physically possible to get to a foreign mission field in a matter of hours. It wasn't that long ago, though, that it would have taken a very long time to arrive at the same location.

D. The great 18th century English preacher George Whitefield was instrumental in bringing revival to England and the American colonies. He made 13 missionary voyages across the Atlantic Ocean in service to the Lord (It's an odd number because he died here). Each trip sailing across the Atlantic Ocean could take between 8 to 12 weeks. That means George Whitefield spent between 2 to 3 years on a ship in the middle of the ocean just to get to the mission field. What do you do during all that time? To get a little insight, take a look at entries from Whitefield's personal journal:

> *The spirit of supplication increases in my heart daily. May it increase more and more.*

> *At night, I and my five companions went upon deck, and interceded and sung psalms, by which my heart was much enlarged.*

> *My heart was much enlarged in prayer, and I can say, the Love of God was shed abroad abundantly therein. For ever adored be the riches of His free mercy!*

> *Lord, enlarge my narrow heart, and give me that charity which rejoices not in iniquity, but in the truth.*

> *Friday, January 13. Set apart this day as a day of humiliation, abstinence, and intercession for friends and all mankind; and found my heart greatly enlarged in that Divine exercise. Intercession is a glorious means to sweeten the heart.*

> *Saturday, Dec. 31. My heart was much enlarged in intercession. The evening*

was exceedingly calm, the sky clear, and all things conspired to praise that glorious and lofty One Who inhabits eternity, who stretcheth forth the heavens like a curtain, and holdeth the waters in the hollow of His hand.[4]
–George Whitefield

E. Rev. Francis Asbury was the father of the American Methodist circuit riders in the 18th and 19th centuries. A disciple of John Wesley, he carried the Gospel relentlessly throughout the frontier of the American colonies (later the United States) for 45 years until his death. In all, Asbury traveled 270,000 miles on horseback.[5] What does a solitary man do in the saddle for all those miles and all those years?

Prayer was a large part of his life. Thus he began every day: 'Rose this morning with a determination to fight or die, and spent an hour in earnest prayer.' Communion with God through prayer was his very life. 'Having a day of rest from public exercises, I spent it in meditation, prayer, and reading.' He was always planning to secure more time for prayer. 'I feel determined to use more private prayer, and may the Lord make me more serious, more watchful, and more holy.' Wherever he stopped for the night he prayed; wherever he ate he closed the meal with prayer. At the approach of Conference he sought opportunities of special prayer for divine guidance.

At one time it was his practice to set apart three hours of every twenty-four for this spiritual exercise; at another period in his life he gave himself to private prayer seven times a day; at another time it was his habit to spend a part of every hour when awake praying; at still another, ten minutes of every hour. When men mocked him his revenge was a prayer that God would bless them. Freeborn Garrettson said of him that he prayed the most and prayed the best of any man he knew. If ever a man sought to live a life of prayer it was he. 'I am much employed in the spirit and duty of prayer, he writes, 'but earnestly desire to be more so. My desire is that prayer should mix with every thought, with every wish, with every word, and with every action, that all might ascend as a holy, acceptable sacrifice to God.'[6] –Ezra Squier Tipple

F. When we look at these historical examples of missionaries and revivalists, we see a clear priority placed on much prayer and its effect on the human heart. Today, the prayer room *is* the most effective mode of travel because it fosters the slow burn of discipleship and being conformed to the image of Christ. It doesn't satisfy our shallow urges for immediate gratification.

G. While missions might benefit practically from the ability to get anywhere

[4] Whitefield, George. *George Whitefield's Journals*. Edinburgh: Banner of Truth Trust, 1960. Print.
[5] "Circuit Riders in Early American Methodism." *Archives & History*. United Methodist Church. Web. 14 July 2016.
[6] Tipple, Ezra Squier. *Francis Asbury: The Prophet of the Long Road*. The Methodist Book Concern, 1916. Print.

quickly, the question remains, "Are the missionaries prepared?"

III. **THE PROGRESS OF THE HEART EQUALS THE PROGRESS OF THE MISSION**

A. Human sentiment and good intentions are inadequate to fulfill the Great Commission. Man-made determination cannot stand in the face of adversity and demonic opposition.

> *Our great need is heart-preparation. Luther held it as an axiom: "He who has prayed well has studied well." We do not say that men are not to think and use their intellects, but he will use his intellect best who cultivates his heart most.*[7] *–E.M. Bounds*

B. Consider the following meditation as you commit to the life-long preparation of your heart for the mission field ahead. Make it a priority for your life to cultivate your heart for the mission—to have its capacity enlarged by God.

> *The heart is the savior of the world. Heads do not save. Genius, brains, brilliancy, strength, natural gifts do not save. The gospel flows through hearts. All the mightiest forces are heart forces. All the sweetest and loveliest graces are heart graces. Great hearts make great characters. Great hearts make divine characters. God is love. There is nothing greater than love. Nothing greater than God. Hearts make heaven. Heaven is love. There is nothing higher, nothing sweeter than heaven. It is the heart and not the head which makes God's great preachers. Head homage does not pass current in heaven. Big hearts make big preachers. Good hearts make good preachers. A theological school to enlarge and cultivate the heart is the golden desire of the gospel.*

> *The good shepherd gives his live for the sheep, but heads never make martyrs. It is the heart which surrenders the life to love and fidelity. It is easier to fill the head, than it is to prepare the heart. It is easier to make a brain sermon than to make a heart sermon. It was heart that drew the son of God from heaven, and it is heart that will draw men to heaven. Men of heart is what the world needs to sympathize with its woe, to kiss away its sorrows, to pity its misery, and to alleviate its pain. Christ was eminently the man of sorrows because he was preeminently the man of heart.*

> *He who does not sow with heart in his study will never reap a harvest in God. The closet is the heart's study. We will learn more about how to preach and what to preach there than we can learn in our libraries. Jesus wept is the shortest and biggest verse in the Bible. It is he who goes forth weeping,*

---

[7] Bounds.

not preaching great sermons, bearing precious seed, who shall come again rejoicing bringing his sheaves with him. Praying gives sense, brings wisdom, broadens and strengthens the mind. The closet is a perfect school teacher and schoolhouse for the preacher. Thought is not only brightened and clarified in prayer, but thought is born in prayer. We can learn more in an hour praying, when praying indeed, than from many hours in study. Book are in the closet which can be found and read nowhere else. Revelations are made in the closet which are made nowhere else. –E.M. Bounds

PRAYER *that* IMPACTS *the* WORLD

RECOMMENDED READING FOR FURTHER STUDY

Forerunners in Praying to Impact the World

Nazirite DNA by Lou Engle (TheCall, 2015)

Rees Howells: Intercessor by Norman Grubb (Christian Literature Crusade, 1952)

Samuel Rees Howells: A Life of Intercession by Richard Maton (ByFaith Media, 2012)

Seeking God in Consecration and Community

The Pursuit of God by A.W. Tozer (Moody Publishers, 1948)

The Rewards of Fasting: Experiencing the Power and Affections of God by Mike Bickle and Dana Candler (Forerunner Publishing, 2005)

Shaping History Through Prayer and Fasting by Derek Prince (Whitaker House, 1973)

Life Together by Dietrich Bonhoeffer (Augsburg Fortress Publishers, 1939)

Gaining a Global Vision

Let the Nations Be Glad! The Supremacy of God in Missions by John Piper (Baker Academic, 1993)

When a Jew Rules the World: What the Bible Really Says about Israel in the Plan of God by Joel Richardson (WND Books, 2015)

An Appeal to Heaven by Dutch Sheets (Dutch Sheets Ministries, 2015)

PRAYER *that* IMPACTS *the* WORLD

ABOUT JUSTICE HOUSE OF PRAYER DC

Who We Are

An evangelical missions organization founded in 2004, Justice House of Prayer DC serves Washington, DC and the nation through ongoing prayer and strategic activism. We are committed to pray for national leaders as we seek spiritual transformation and cultural reformation to be established from the governmental gate of our nation's capital.

Our History

In 2004, the Lord led Lou Engle and a large group of young people to journey from Colorado Springs to fast and pray in Washington, DC with a focus on the upcoming elections. An ongoing chorus of prayer and worship was birthed from those initial 50 days; the Justice House of Prayer DC was born.

Following soon after with their family, Matt Lockett and his wife Kim have provided leadership to JHOP DC since 2005.

Join Us in Washington, DC

Strategically located only blocks away from the Supreme Court and the U.S. Capitol, Justice House of Prayer DC facilitates corporate prayer, teaching and training through young adult internships and a growing community of intercessors. The prayer room is open to the public during regularly scheduled hours, posted online.

Our hope is in Jesus Christ, the one whom Scripture declares is "the Desire of all nations" (Haggai 2:7). He is worthy of our extravagant love and devotion. Unceasing ministry to the Lord is the center of all we do, the platform for unity and spiritual authority in all activities. Learn more about this community of contending prayer at JHOPDC.com

Our Partnership

This book was birthed from a partnership between JHOP DC and the International House of Prayer–Tallahassee, a missions base serving the capital city of Florida. Founded in 2005, IHOP-TLH is devoted to night and day prayer for the fulfillment of the Great Commission and the return of Jesus. Learn more at IHOPTLH.org

37857912R00100

Made in the USA
San Bernardino, CA
26 August 2016